onions onions onions

P9-DFB-436

onions onions onions

Rosemary Moon

FIREFLY BOOKS

A FIREFLY BOOK

Published by Firefly Books Ltd. 2000

Copyright © 2000 Quintet Publishing Limited

All rights reserved. No part of this publication may be
reproduced, stored in a retieval system or transmitted
in any form or by any means, electronic, mechanical,
photocopying, recording or otherwise, without the
prior written permission of the publisher.

First Printing

Canadian Cataloguing in Publication Data

Moon, Rosemary
Onions, onions, onions: globe, spanish, vidalia, walla walla, shallot, in a wave of flavor and aroma
Includes index.
ISBN: 1-55209-364-6
1. Cookery (Onions). 2. Onions.   I. Title.
TX803.05M66 2000   641.6'525   C99-931650-8

U.S. Cataloguing in Publication Data

Moon, Rosemary
Onions, onions, onions: globe, spanish, vidalia, walla walla, shallot, in a wave of flavor and aroma
Rosemary Moon, 1st ed   [144]p: col, Ill : cm
Includes index.
Summary: Over 80 recipes using onions in cuisines from around the world.
ISBN: 1-55209-364-6
1. Cookery (Onions). 2. Onions.   I. Title.
641.6/525–dc21   2000   CIP

Published in Canada in 2000 by
Firefly Books Ltd.
3680 Victoria Park Avenue
Willowdale, Ontario
M2H 3K1

Published in the United States in 2000 by
Firefly Books (U.S.) Inc.
P.O. Box 1338, Ellicott Station
Buffalo, New York
14205

This book was designed and produced by
Quintet Publishing Ltd.
6 Blundell Street
London N7 9BH

Creative Director: Richard Dewing
Art Director: Paula Marchant
Design: Paul Wright
Project Editor: Debbie Foy
Editor: Anna Bennett

Typeset in Great Britain by
Central Southern Typesetters, Eastbourne
Manufactured in Malaysia by CH Color Scan Sdn. Bhd.
Printed in China by Leefung-Asco Printers Ltd.

Picture Credits
Seaspring Photos: p8, 19, 20, 21; ET Archive: p10, p11, p12; Life File: p5, p14

*This book is for Tony, who loves onions, and for Pat,
for all the tears and especially the happy ones.*

Contents

Acknowledgments

There are many people who should be thanked for their roles in the production of the book. My husband Nick is always enthusiastic about my food and, bless him, even seems to cope when there is the occasional need to eat onions for breakfast! The herring and onion salad went down a treat at 7.30 am! Toby Moon, our much-loved gourmand Shetland Sheepdog, was less enthusiastic about this project than some (a book on cheese would be his idea of heaven), but he was introduced to herring roe for breakfast through that very same salad and – I can tell you – herring roe is one of the things that Shelties like best.

So often a cookbook is judged on its photographs and those in this volume are truly mouthwatering. So special thanks are due to Tim Ferguson-Hill, the photographer, and to Emma Patmore, the home economist and food stylist. I know what long days the team worked and I am delighted with the results – thank you both.

My great thanks are due to my horticultural friends at West Dean Gardens near Chichester in Sussex, England. Sarah Wain explained all sorts of matters horticultural in her patient Melbourne manner, and Stuart the Champion Onion Man might have gossiped away rather too many of his top tips for prize-winning onions. Their time was generously given and much appreciated.

We have a marvelous bunch of friends who are always happy to munch their way through recipe tests, kindly commenting and suggesting the occasional tweak. Those who have done sterling eating work on this project include: Mum and Dad Noble who tackled some of the richer dishes with relish and pronounced them delicious; Jimbo and Sarah from West Dean; Sue from down the road; James and Sarah; and Dawn and Martin over the road, who are quite new in the village and think recipe testing is an excellent idea. And to everyone else who has gathered round the dining table – thank you all.

Rosemary Moon.

about the onion

Many pieces of silver were spent on the purchase of onions to feed the laborers building the Great Pyramids of Egypt. Without onions, the Seven Wonders of the World might only have been six. This chapter details the global history of the onion, as well as exploring the many varieties available to the home cook.

Chives, with their purple flower heads almost ready to burst open, make a decorative and unusual edging to flower and vegetable borders.

introduction

The onion is one of the oldest vegetables known to man and an essential ingredient in just about every cuisine of the world. It is hard to imagine a vegetable basket without onions for they are the basis of so many different recipes.

Onions are edible alliums, or lilies. Many varieties exist, all of which are edible, but only a certain number are commonly used for culinary purposes, because some of the more decorative varieties are bitter-tasting and, although not actually poisonous, are simply not palatable. Today, as more and more people look for natural healing remedies, onions are also keenly popular for their medicinal properties. Alliums are also very beautiful in the garden, where their decorative heads form a spectacular display. I always leave one or two leeks and onions to go to seed, giving me a display of large purple flower heads.

This book explores the versatility of the onion. When I was asked to write it I thought it sounded like a pretty straightforward general cookbook. However, a week or so into the recipe testing and I was amazed at just

how easy it is to make the onion the star of the dish! Not just by upping the quantities so that it dominates, but by cooking the onions slowly to draw out the delicious sweetness that is onions, a flavor unknown to anyone who simply fries them quickly at the beginning of a dish before adding other ingredients.

Raw, sliced, sautéed, chopped, stewed, pickled, roasted, or baked – however an onion is cooked it is a delight and an essential, not only for infinitely variable international cuisine, but also for a healthy and flavorful diet. And what of the occasional tears? Well, that's a small price to pay. Experiment and enjoy!

The scent of wild garlic often greets you long before the plants, with their delicate white flowers, come into view.

The Egyptians treasured their onions, which were as likely to be seized by their enemies as gold or silver.

The onion *in history*

Onions and their relatives have been grown since humans started to cultivate the land. They were an essential part of the diet of the slaves who built the Great Pyramids in Egypt. One of the pyramids built in 2500 B.C. includes an inscription revealing that onions, garlic, and radishes had been purchased with silver to feed the workers. Although this was a great expense, it was deemed necessary both to keep the workforce healthy and to keep them motivated and working well. Onions of various forms are also depicted in murals in Egyptian and other ancient tombs. Some of the color washes for these paintings would have been made from steeped onion skins, just as the color was used to dye cloth until comparatively recent times.

The Bible is full of references to onions. One of the earliest is the Israelites bemoaning their poor diet after they fled from Egypt, citing the fish which they had enjoyed with cucumbers and onions, among other vegetables. Almost two thousand years later, at the time of the Roman Empire, historians were writing of onions as essential vegetables to be grown in market gardens to supply the

townspeople. By this time, the first century A.D., onions were grown widely throughout the known world – the Roman Empire and Asia, including China, but they were unknown, even in any wild form, in the Americas and Australia. Whether the Romans actually introduced them throughout Europe I do not know, but they did take a great number of their foods with them as they expanded the Roman Empire northward, so they may well have introduced garlic even if onions were already flourishing.

Foods enjoy heights and depths of popularity and fashion. Garlic chives, for example, are a mildly garlic-flavored variety of chive, most certainly a member of the onion family. A relatively new introduction to my herb garden, these aromatic leaves, also called Chinese chives, are known to have existed in China from at least 500 B.C., when they were offered in sacrifice with lamb. They soon featured in Japanese culinary records as well, but it seems to have been many years before they reached the West.

Although many members of the onion family are known to exist in the wild – elephant garlic often grows freely near the sites of early Christian monasteries, possibly having self-perpetuated after a period of cultivation by the monks, and leeks were still found in the wild quite recently, especially in Ireland – onions themselves are now only cultivated. Like wheat and many other essential basic commodities, it is thought that onions originated in the area to the west and north of India and spread through cultivation to all other parts of the temperate and subtropical world with the early explorers and settlers. This is how many crops were established, although varieties that grew well in one place were not always a success in another area.

Onions reach the New Worlds

Christopher Columbus is credited with introducing onions to the Americas at the end of the fifteenth century. Legend has it that the name Chicago is a derivation of a Native American word meaning rotting or smelly onions and Chicago has certainly always been a major onion-growing area.

Onions were introduced to Australia by the first English settlers in 1787. They took onion seeds and sets (small bulbs grown from seed the previous season) with them, regarding them as culinary essentials. By the end of the eighteenth century this most versatile of vegetables was known worldwide. Much work was still to be done, however, in producing the correct cultivars for growing in such an enormous variety of climatic conditions.

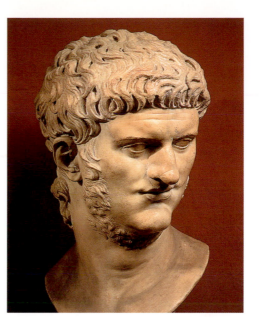

The Emperor Nero. Onions were an essential crop in Rome for feeding the townspeople and were grown extensively in market gardens.

Onions played an important role in the legendary Roman banquets, depicted in this second-century A.D. pavement mosaic.

The onion *family*

The onion family also includes garlic, leeks, and chives but this book focuses primarily on the onion and its many uses in cooking, both as a central and supporting ingredient. Here, however, is a brief introduction to the onion's relatives:

Chives are a must in any herb garden, and are usually grown there rather than in the main vegetable beds as they are ideally suited to alpine slopes and rocky crevices. Only the leaves and flowers are eaten, not the bulb. The leaves, delicately onion-flavored, should be snipped with scissors. Leave chives to self-seed in cracks on your garden steps: their little purple flower heads are attractive to look at and also taste good in salads. Chives are more widely grown than any other type of edible allium as they can withstand most climatic conditions. The name chive derives from the Latin *cepa* and was originally used to describe any small plant of the onion family. **Garlic chives** are used in the same way as common chives, although they are stronger in flavor. Known since ancient times in China, where this plant originates, these chives add a very special flavor to salads. Garlic chives are larger than the common chive and they make impressive edging plants.

Garlic is almost a cult vegetable and is, in my opinion, much maligned through over-use. Like a glimpse of stocking, it should be much more of a suggestion than a blatant flavor statement. Used too heavily it can be

unpleasant but added subtly to a dish it can introduce an interesting flavor. A clove rubbed around a salad bowl or over toasted bread is heavenly.

Onion Weed and **Ramsons** are easy to confuse. The flower stems of the former are triangular in shape and have a white flower. Onion weed naturalizes quickly and invasively and is as likely to be found on a wooded foreshore as it is by streams and in other damp, shady places. Ramsons is the traditional name for wild garlic and is native to the UK and northern Europe. Although ramsons usually grows by streams and in wooded areas, the fashionable area of Ramsons Dock in south London would suggest that the plant might once have been found in abundance along the banks of the River Thames. Confusion between ramsons and onion weed occurs as both plants have a similar habitat and white flowers – the stem is the most helpful identification pointer for non-botanists.

Welsh Onions are more commonly, if incorrectly, known as **Scallions**, **Green Onions**, or **Spring Onions**. The confusion arises as spring onion is not a true term, but is often used for Welsh onions, the species *Alluim fistulosum*, which are harvested early when small and are thought to have been introduced into northern Europe through Russia from China. It is possible that the term derives from the Anglo-Saxon *waelise* or the German *welsch*, meaning foreign. They are the best salad onions and are commonly used raw, although many people prefer to cook them lightly, especially in stir-fries.

Leeks are a great vegetable for gardeners and cooks alike. They are as versatile as onions, survive well in the garden throughout a temperate winter and grow tall, erect, and branching, providing almost architectural plants in the flower borders. As ancient as onions, leeks were certainly spread throughout Europe by the Romans who were very partial to this vegetable. It is said that the Emperor Nero ate leeks to improve his singing voice. The leek is the national emblem of Wales, and is popularly thought to have become so as Welsh soldiers wore a leek pinned to their clothes as a mark of identification, so that they did not kill each other in battle. It is interesting to note that the Welsh name for daffodils, the other national mascot, is *Cenin Pedr*, or St. Peter's Leek.

Shallots are less widely grown by amateur gardeners than onions, and yet they provide good results and yield from a small area. They are also part of a great gardening heritage and store well throughout the winter. Shallots are valuable to cooks as they provide a great deal of flavor from very little bulk – they are ideal for sauces and for incorporating into pastry and dough. In the garden they

Welsh

Shallots

Mild

Pickling

Spanish

White

Red

Oso

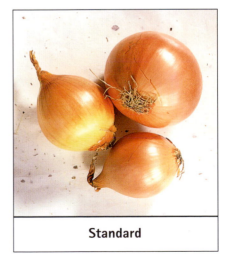

Standard

Cooking *with onions*

An ingredient as versatile as an onion may be cooked in a number of ways to fulfil its culinary potential.

Sautéing or Frying is usually done in oil or butter and is the classic way to begin a large number of recipes. Some call for the onions to be quickly softened to a state of translucency, but you will find that the longer this takes the better (15 to 20 minutes is ideal) because this releases the natural sweetness of the onions.

Puréeing is really a preparation rather than a cooking method. Onions are blended to a thick paste to be fried, usually after spices, as the basis of many Indian, Thai, and Pacific Rim dishes. The puréed onions form not only the main ingredient but also the thickener for the sauce.

Baking may be done in or out of the skins, although the skins will help to hold the onions together during cooking. Most onions to be baked should be par-cooked first.

Roasting is a fashionable way of cooking onions (and many root vegetables) at high temperatures in a little olive oil for flavor. Roasting produces a deliciously caramelized outer crust that is sweet to the taste.

Boiling is a good way of softening onions which are going to be finished in another way, e.g. in a sauce, topped with bread crumbs and broiled. Leave small onions whole, or chop large ones into big chunks.

Braising in a little broth or gravy produces an almost pot-roasted effect.

Deep-frying is usually reserved for onion rings, either floured or battered. These are a classic accompaniment to steaks.

Onions are an essential ingredient in chutneys, savory fruit sauces, and salads as well as in casseroles.

Easy *onion flavors*

There are a number of ways of adding extra onion flavor to dishes without actually using onions. One of the easiest is dried onion soup mix, which is great in breads, scones, and mixed into bread crumbs for crisp toppings. Onion-flavored salt is good sprinkled over salads – try it also over tomatoes on toast. Onion broth can be bought, but I often make my own, by simmering onion skins in water with a few seasonings, especially if I have been using a lot of onions. This broth is very useful and goes well in almost any dish.

Complementary foods and flavors

A few very basic foods and flavorings are natural partners to onions. One is cheese – try strong yellow onions with a robust Cheddar, or sweet Vidalias with a sweet nutty Swiss cheese such as Emmenthal. Olives and onions go well together, and anchovies are also a very worthy partner. My favorite support herbs for onions are thyme, either common or lemon, and bay leaf. A good spice is mace (the aromatic outer casing of the nutmeg).

Nutty Swiss Emmenthal cheese is especially good with a sweet white onion such as Vidalia.

How to chop *an onion properly*

This is one of the most basic skills to learn in the kitchen. I always try to leave the root intact while chopping, and it is essential to use a very sharp knife, preferably with a large blade, to do this properly.

1. Peel off the papery skin, chopping off the top of the onion but leaving the root intact. Cut in half through the onion and the root.

2. Place the onion on a board, cut side down, and slice crosswise toward the root, but not right up to it, making three, four, or five cuts, depending on the size of the onion.

3. Now cut lengthwise, again not right through to the root, three, four, or five times.

4. Finally cut crosswise again, across the onion, slicing it finely. As you do so, the onion should fall onto the board in neat dice until you reach the root. Chop any flesh left around the root, then discard it.

What to drink *with onions*

An ingredient of such eclectic usage is difficult to match too specifically to a particular style of wine or beer and it is best to accompany your chosen onion dish with your favorite tipple. Most onion dishes are fairly robust, however, and demand a drink which will not be lost or overwhelmed. My preference in wines is for reds, and most grape varieties will match onion cuisine well. The traditional casseroles and stews of regional France are all served with the local wines, and purists would argue that a Beef Bourguignon should never be drunk with anything other than a Burgundy, although such rigidity is becoming a thing of the past. Choose a full-bodied red such as Cabernet Sauvignon, Merlot, or a country red for stews and casseroles, whereas a lighter Gamay, Chinon, or Zinfandel will sit well with onion-based vegetarian dishes. That said, a robust and full-bodied red with a touch of challenging roughness, such as a Burgundy, is necessary to stand up to the bold richness of a *Pissaladière* (page 128). White wines should be full-flavored and the ever-popular Chardonnay, especially if oaked, will complement most onion dishes extremely well, although I would suggest a lighter, crisper Sauvignon blanc with many spicier, lighter dishes and onion-topped salads.

Many rich Belgian and Flemish beers go well with onion-based dishes, whereas English dark beers are great with rich casseroles and pies. Together, beer and onions produce wonderful flavors in slow-cooked dishes and are also natural partners to cheese and onion-flavored breads, or pies to be served with salads and pickles. Beer, onions, and bread are a classic combination as is seen in the popularity of English pub food, especially Ploughman's Lunches (page 130).

A simple lunch of salad, cheese, bread, and onions is best washed down with a glass of beer.

sauces, pickles, and stuffings

Onions are the essential ingredient in so many pickles and sauces, adding relish and flavor to main dishes and entrées. Slow simmered for depth of flavor, or bound into a forcemeat of crumbs and herbs, the onion is an excellent supporting ingredient.

sweet onion *and apple chutney*

*Makes about 4 lb
(1.8 kg)*

3¼ lb (1.5 kg) onions, chopped
3¼ lb (1.5 kg) cooking apples,
  peeled, cored, and diced
3 cups (700 mL) golden raisins
Grated rind and juice of
  2 lemons
1¾ lb (750 g) brown sugar
2½ cups (600 mL) distilled
  malt vinegar

A mild, fruity chutney containing no spices at all. Try it in cheese sandwiches, with cheese on toast, and with meat dishes such as shepherd's pie.

Preparation time: 30 minutes Cooking time: 1 hour

Place all the ingredients in a large preserving pot and heat gently until the sugar has dissolved, stirring all the time.

Bring to a boil, and allow to simmer for 30 to 40 minutes or until thickened with all the liquid absorbed.

Meanwhile, scrub preserving jars in hot, soapy water, then rinse thoroughly. Heat jars at 350°F (180°C) for 15 minutes.

Pour chutney mixture into jars immediately, seal, and label. This chutney does not need to mature and will keep well for about a year.

traditional *pickled onions*

*Makes about 2¼ lb
(1 kg)*

2¼ lb (1 kg) pickling onions
  or small shallots
½ cup (125 mL) sea salt
1 quart (1L) water
½ cup (125 mL) sugar,
  preferably unrefined
1 quart (1L) malt vinegar
2 Tbsp (25 mL) pickling spice
  or coriander seeds

I'm sure it's peeling the onions that puts people off pickling their own!

Pouring boiling water over the onions and leaving them for 5 minutes prior to peeling can make the skins easier to slip off. I add sugar to my onions because I like them slightly sweet, but it's not essential.

Preparation time: 20 minutes, plus 2 days for brining
Spicing and filling time: 2½ hours for vinegar; 10-15 minutes to fill the jars

Cut a small slice from each end of the onions, place them in a bowl, and cover with boiling water. Leave for 5 minutes, then drain the onions and run them under cold water until cool enough to handle. Slip off the skins.

Stir the salt into the water until dissolved, then pour the brine over the onions in a mixing bowl. Put a plate on the onions in the bowl, to stop them bobbing up out of the brine. Cover and leave for 48 hours – any less and the onions will be soft; some pickling experts say 3 days, but I find 2 days is right.

Place the sugar, vinegar, and spice in a covered pan and bring almost to a boil. Stir to ensure the sugar is dissolved, cover, then leave for 2 hours, or until the vinegar is cold. Strain to remove the spices.

Drain and thoroughly rinse the onions, then pack them tightly into clean pickle jars – really push them in. Add enough cold vinegar to completely cover the onions.

Seal the jars with screw-on lids, then label. Leave to mature for at least one month before eating.

sauces, pickles,
and stuffings

sweet onion and apple chutney

walnut *and onion chutney*

*Makes about
2 ¼ lb (1 Kg)*

2¼ lb (1 kg) onions, sliced thin
4 Tbsp (50 mL) olive oil
1 lb 2 oz (500 g) apples,
  peeled, cored, and chopped
1 cup (250 mL) red wine
1 cup (250 mL) sugar,
  preferably unrefined
2 tsp (10 mL) coarse sea salt
1 tsp (5 mL) black pepper
⅓ cup (100 mL) red wine
  vinegar
2 cups (450 mL) walnut pieces
Lemon juice to taste

A cross between a traditional chutney and the now-fashionable onion marmalades, the texture of this relish combines the crunch of nuts with a fruity onion base. It should be treated like a marmalade, and kept in the fridge once opened. Eat within 3 to 4 weeks.

Preparation time: 15 minutes Cooking time: 1¼ hours

Cook the onions in the oil in a large deep skillet for 10 minutes until well softened, then add the apples and red wine. Simmer for 20 minutes, until both the onions and apples are well cooked.

Stir in the sugar, salt and pepper, and vinegar and cook for a further 30 minutes, until the chutney is thickened and most of the liquid has been absorbed.

Add the walnuts and lemon juice and stir them evenly throughout the mixture. Continue cooking for a further 10 minutes until all the liquid has gone.

Scrub preserving jars in hot, soapy water, then rinse thoroughly. Heat jars at 350°F (180°C) for 15 minutes. Pack chutney mixture into the jars, seal, and label.

onion *sauce*

Serves 4 to 6

3 to 4 large onions, cut into
  6 or 8 segments depending
  on size
6 black peppercorns
1 bay leaf
4 Tbsp (50 mL) butter
3 Tbsp (45 mL) flour
1 cup (250 mL) milk
Salt and black pepper

Another culinary classic, this goes very well with roast lamb. Any leftovers always mix well with cold meat in pilafs or shepherd's pie. I like to leave my onions in large segments, to give the sauce texture. You can use all onion water if you prefer, and add 3–4 tablespoons (45–50 mL) powdered dried milk to it.

Preparation time: 15 minutes Cooking time: 10 minutes

Place the onions in a saucepan with the peppercorns and bay and just enough cold water to cover. Bring to a boil, then cover and simmer for 10 minutes. Drain the onions, reserving the water, and discard the peppercorns and bay leaf.

Heat the butter, flour, milk, and 1 cup (250 mL) of the onion water together in the pan, stirring all the time. Bring to a boil, then add the drained onions and cook for a further 2 to 3 minutes. Add a little more onion liquor if the sauce is too thick.

Season to taste and serve with roast lamb.

walnut and onion chutney

onion *and olive sauce*

Serves 4

3 large onions, sliced fine
4 Tbsp (50 mL) olive oil
Salt and black pepper
3 to 4 large sprigs thyme
Fine grated zest and juice of
  1 lemon
1 cup (250 mL) fish or
  vegetable broth
12 juicy green olives, pitted
  and chopped
4 Tbsp (50 mL) anchovy fillets,
  drained and chopped fine
2 Tbsp (25 mL) chopped parsley

This is a rich sauce to serve with meaty fish such as tuna or swordfish.

I like to add anchovies to cut through the richness, but leave them out

if you must. The longer you cook this the better.

Preparation time: 10 minutes Cooking time: 35 minutes

Toss the onions in the oil in a large skillet, then add plenty of salt and pepper, the leaves from the thyme, and the lemon zest. Cook over medium heat for 20 minutes until the onions are well softened and starting to brown.

Add the broth, bring to a boil, and simmer gently for 5 to 10 minutes until just slightly reduced.

Stir in the olives and anchovies, then season the sauce to taste, adding the parsley and lemon juice at the last moment. Served with broiled fish steaks.

red onion *and shallot marmalade*

*Makes about 2 lb
(900 g)*

2¼ lb (1 kg) red onions
2 cups (225mL) shallots
⅓ cup (100 mL) olive oil
6 large sprigs thyme
1 cup (250 mL) granulated
  sugar, unrefined if possible
2 tsp (10 mL) coarse sea salt
1 tsp (5 mL) black pepper
⅓ cup (100 mL) sherry vinegar
1½ cups (350 mL) Oloroso
  sherry
Lemon juice to taste

A condiment for garnishing chops and steaks and to serve with cold meats

and cheese. The marmalade keeps for about a month in the refrigerator.

Preparation time: 15 minutes Cooking time: 1½ hours

Thinly slice the peeled onions and shallots – the slicing attachment on a food processor does this with the minimum of tears.

Heat the oil in a large deep skillet, add the onions, shallots, and thyme and cook for 25 to 30 minutes, until well softened.

Stir in the sugar, salt, and pepper and cook for a further 10 minutes, then add the vinegar and sherry.

Simmer the marmalade for 30 to 40 minutes, until it is thick and most of the liquid has reduced. Season to taste with lemon juice.

Pack into freshly sterilized jars, then seal and label. Refrigerate after opening.

sauces, pickles,
and stuffings

red onion and shallot marmalade

scallion *and parsley sauce*

This is cream-based and rather richer than a traditional white sauce, but it is bright in taste and color and is excellent with white fish like roast cod or broiled skate.

Preparation time: 10 minutes Cooking time: 10 minutes

Cook the whites of the onions in the oil in a small skillet for 6 to 8 minutes over medium heat until well softened – add the chile with the scallions if using.

Pour in the cream and bring the sauce to a boil. Simmer for 2 to 3 minutes, until the cream is just starting to reduce.

Stir in the shredded scallion greens and the parsley, then season to taste. Add any fish liquor that you have, then serve the sauce spooned over the fish.

Serves 4 to 6

8 to 10 scallions, the whites chopped fine and the greens shredded lengthwise

2 Tbsp (25 mL) peanut or sunflower oil

1 green chile, chopped fine (optional)

1 cup (250 mL) heavy cream

1 large handful (about 5 Tbsp/65 mL), freshly chopped flat leaf parsley

Salt and paprika

sage and *red onion stuffing*

Serves 4 to 6

2 large handfuls fresh sage

2 large red onions, chopped
  very fine

4 Tbsp (50 mL) butter

3 cups (700 mL) fresh white
  bread crumbs

Salt and black pepper

1 large egg, beaten

This is one of the classic stuffing or forcemeat mixtures, traditionally served with pork. Commercial stuffings are generally made with dried sage and, to my taste, lack color and pungency. Fresh herbs and a strong onion flavor are essential.

Preparation time: 25 minutes Cooking time: 30 minutes

Pour boiling water over the sage leaves in a bowl and leave to stand for 10 minutes.

Fry the onions gently in the butter for about 10 minutes until well softened, then add them and all their juices to the bread crumbs in a large bowl.

Drain the sage, shake the leaves, then pat dry on paper towels. Chop very fine and add to the onions and bread crumbs with plenty of seasoning.

Add just enough egg to make a moist stuffing that will hold together. Use either to fill a joint of pork, or roll the stuffing into 12 balls. If the stuffing is to be cooked separately, coat the balls in oil or melted butter, then roast them in a hot oven at 400°F (200°C) for 30 minutes, turning and basting them once.

spiced chickpea *and onion stuffing*

This is a marvelous stuffing to use in a shoulder of lamb.

Ask your butcher to remove the blade bone, then use this stuffing

to fill the cavity. Spice the lamb with ground cumin and

allspice and you'll have a very exotic roast.

Serves 4 to 6

1 large red onion
6 to 8 scallions, chopped fine
2 Tbsp (50 mL) chili or peanut
  oil
1 tsp (5 mL) mild chili powder
1 medium eggplant, diced fine
14 fl oz (398 mL) canned
  chickpeas (garbanzos),
  drained
Salt and black pepper

Preparation time: 20 minutes

Cook the onions in the oil with the chili powder for 10 minutes, or until softened. Add the eggplant and cook for a further 5 minutes.

Turn the drained chickpeas into a bowl and mash them lightly with the back of a fork. Add the onion and eggplant mixture and stir it throughout the chickpeas. Season well, then use to stuff lamb. This stuffing needs to be cooked in meat as it will not hold together to be roasted in balls.

lemongrass, cilantro, *and onion stuffing*

Serves 4 to 6

2 large red onions, chopped
    fine
2 Tbsp (25 mL) peanut oil
Pinch chili powder
2 stalks lemongrass, bruised
    and chopped very fine
3 cups (700 mL) fresh white
    bread crumbs
2 big handfuls chopped cilantro
Salt and black pepper
1 large egg, beaten
4 Tbsp (50 mL) butter, melted
Chopped cilantro to garnish

I like to serve this with baked pork chops. I love stuffings when the outside is crisp, but the inside holds a surprise flavor such as lemongrass.

Preparation time: 25 minutes Cooking time: 30 minutes

Preheat the oven to 400°F (200°C).

Cook the onions in the oil with the chili and lemongrass for 8 to 10 minutes until well softened. Allow to cool slightly.

Mix the bread crumbs with the cilantro in a large bowl, then season well. Stir the spiced onions throughout the mixture, add the beaten egg, then mix to bind the stuffing together. Add a little melted butter if necessary to keep the mixture together.

Shape the stuffing into 12 balls – wet your hands with cold water to make the shaping easier.

Melt the butter in a suitable roasting pan on the stove, then add the stuffing balls and turn them in the butter until completely coated. Roast in the hot oven for about 30 minutes, until a deep golden brown. Sprinkle with extra cilantro and serve with oven-baked pork chops.

soups, appetizers, and hors d'oeuvres

The star of the starter, or an essential background flavoring?
Onions can dominate and enrich soups and starters, or be
used as a piquant last-minute garnish.

french onion *soup*

Serves 6

1 Tbsp (15 mL) butter

2 Tbsp (25 mL) olive oil

4 large onions, sliced fine

3 cups (700mL) beef or
   vegetable broth

Salt and black pepper

3 to 4 large bay leaves

6 thick slices French bread

3/4 cup (170 mL) grated Swiss
   cheese

The traditional hangover-remedy soup, sold in all-night cafés in Paris to revive revelers in the early hours of the morning. Some people thicken this soup with flour, but I like it just as it is.

Preparation time: 30–40 minutes Cooking time: 30–40 minutes

Heat the butter and oil together in a large pot, add the onions, and cook over medium heat for about 20 to 30 minutes until well browned but not burned.

Add the broth to the pot, along with the seasonings. Bring to a boil, cover, and simmer for 30 minutes.

Remove the bay leaves, then season again to taste.

Place the bread, either in the soup in a heatproof serving dish, or on a broiler rack. Scatter with the cheese and broil until just browned. Serve the toasted bread and cheese over the soup.

lebanese onion *and couscous soup*

Serves 6

4 large onions, sliced fine

2 Tbsp (25 mL) oil

1 Tbsp (15 mL) butter

1 red chile, seeded and
   chopped fine

1 tsp (5 mL) mild chili powder

1/2 tsp (2 mL) turmeric

1 tsp (5 mL) ground coriander

8 cups (2 L) vegetable or
   chicken broth

Salt and black pepper

1/3 cup (80 mL) couscous

Similar to French Onion soup but with extra spice, especially good for really cold days.

Preparation time: 20 minutes Cooking time: 40 minutes

Cook the onions in the oil and butter until well browned – this will take about 15 minutes over medium heat.

Stir in the chopped chile and the spices and cook over low heat for a further 1 to 2 minutes before adding the broth. Season lightly then bring to a boil. Cover and simmer for 30 minutes.

Stir the couscous into the soup, bring back to a boil, and simmer for a further 10 minutes. Season to taste and serve immediately.

french onion soup

cauliflower *and scallion soup*

Serves 4 to 6

1 bunch scallions (about 8
   to 10), trimmed
2 Tbsp (25 mL) butter
1 large potato, peeled and
   diced
1 large cauliflower, chopped
   (including the stalk)
5 cups (1.2 L) water
Salt and black pepper
1 cup (250 mL) milk, or more

A thick vegetable soup, the green onion tops providing an appealing garnish.

No herbs, spices, or broth are required – the flavor of the cauliflower and the onions is more than enough.

Preparation time: 10 minutes Cooking time: 30 minutes

Reserve the green tops of the scallions. Chop the white part and add to the butter in a pot and cook slowly for 5 minutes, until the onions are softened.

Stir in the potato and cauliflower, cover, and cook over low heat for a further 5 minutes, shaking the pot from time to time.

Add the water with the salt and pepper and bring to a boil. Cover the pot, then simmer for 20 minutes.

Remove from the heat and allow the soup to cool slightly then purée until smooth. Return to the stove and add the milk, thinning the soup to the required consistency. Reheat gently, seasoning to taste.

Finely chop the reserved green onion tops and stir into the soup just before serving.

chilled scallion *and cucumber soup*

Its lively flavors make this a soup to be enjoyed by everyone, even those who claim not to like chilled soups.

Serves 6

Preparation time: 1½ hours, including cooling time Chilling time: about 2 hours

Reserve a few of the green scallion tops for garnish, then place the remaining onions, lemongrass, chiles, and lime leaves in a large pot with the crumbled bouillon cube. Add the water, then bring to a boil. Add the cucumber, cover the pot, and remove it immediately from the heat. Allow to marinate for 1 hour.

Purée the soup until smooth, then press the mixture through a fine sieve with the back of a ladle. Whisk in the yogurt and fish sauce, then season to taste with a little salt if necessary. Chill thoroughly for at least 2 hours.

Add the reserved chopped scallion tops to the soup just before serving, and spoon the soup over a tablespoon or so of crushed ice in each bowl to serve.

6 large scallions, trimmed and
  sliced
1 stalk lemongrass, bruised and
  chopped fine
2 green chiles and 2 caribe
  chiles, or 3 green chiles,
  seeded and chopped fine
2 lime leaves or finely grated
  rind of 1 lime
1 vegetable bouillon cube,
  crumbled
4 cups (850 mL) water
1 large cucumber, seeded and
  chopped
1 cup (250 mL) plain yogurt
1 Tbsp (15 mL) fish sauce
Salt to taste

roasted red onion *and pepper soup*

Serves 4 to 6

2 large red onions, peeled and
  halved
1 large red bell pepper and
  1 large green bell pepper
Salt and black pepper
About 4–5 Tbsp (50–65 mL)
  olive oil
14 fl oz (398 mL) canned
  chopped tomatoes
3 cups (700 mL) vegetable or
  chicken broth
Handful basil leaves
2 Tbsp (25 mL) pesto or
  tapénade (black olive paste)
Shavings of Parmesan cheese
  to serve

Redolent in flavors of the Mediterranean, this rich soup is a meal in itself served with crusty bread.

Preparation time: 1 hour Cooking time: 20 minutes

Preheat the oven to 425°F (220°C). Place the onions and peppers on a baking sheet, season lightly then drizzle with a little olive oil. Roast for about 40 minutes, until the peppers are blackened – turn them once during cooking. Cover the peppers with a damp dish towel and leave for 10 minutes or so, once cooked – this helps to steam loose the skins.

Peel and core the peppers, then roughly chop them with the onions. Cook in the remaining oil for 2 to 3 minutes, then add the tomatoes and broth. Bring to a boil then add the basil and seasonings. Cover and simmer for 15 minutes.

Purée the soup until smooth, return to the pot, and reheat gently if necessary, seasoning to taste. Add a little more broth or water if the soup is too thick.

Swirl the pesto or *tapénade* into the soup, and garnish with Parmesan shavings just before serving.

english-style *onion soup*

Serves 4 to 6

4 Tbsp (57 mL) butter
1 Tbsp (15 mL) olive oil
3 large onions, sliced fine
2 Tbsp (25 mL) flour
5 cups (1.2 L) vegetable broth
Salt and black pepper
½ tsp (2 mL) ground mace
1 cup (250 mL) milk
Lemon juice to taste

A smooth flavorful soup that's great after a digging session in the garden.

Preparation time: 30-40 minutes Cooking time: 30-40 minutes

Heat the butter and oil together in a large pot, add the onions, and cook over moderate heat for about 20 minutes, until well browned. It is important to brown and not burn the onions, and to achieve a good rich chestnut-brown color, or the soup will be insipid.

Stir in the flour, then cook for 2 to 3 minutes until well browned before gradually stirring in the broth.

Bring to a boil, add the seasonings, cover, and cook for 30 to 40 minutes.

Stir in the milk then season the soup to taste, adding a little lemon juice. Reheat gently and serve with crusty bread and strong cheese.

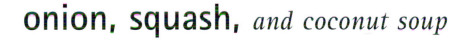

onion, squash, *and coconut soup*

This smooth, spicy soup has a very unusual flavor.

The yogurt provides a cooling garnish.

Serves 4 to 6

Preparation time: 15 minutes Cooking time: 40 minutes

Cook the onions in the oil in a covered pan for 10 minutes, until softened but not browned. Add the squash and cook for a further 5 minutes.

Stir in the lemongrass, chiles, and lime leaves or shredded rind, then add the broth and bring to a boil. Season lightly, cover, and simmer for 20 minutes, or until the squash is tender.

Cool slightly, add the coconut milk and fish sauce, then blend the soup to a smooth purée. Season to taste with salt – if you have left the chile seeds in it is very unlikely you will need pepper!

Serve with a spoonful of plain yogurt and chopped cilantro.

2 large onions, sliced

2 Tbsp (25 mL) sunflower or
   peanut oil

4 cups (900 mL) prepared
   squash, such as butternut,
   diced fine

1 to 2 stalks lemongrass,
   chopped fine

3 small red chiles, seeded if
   wished and chopped fine

3 kaffir lime leaves finely grated
   or shredded rind of 2 limes

5 cups (1.2 L) vegetable broth

Salt and black pepper

1/2 cup (125 mL) coconut milk
   or cream

2 Tbsp (25 mL) fish sauce

Yogurt and chopped cilantro
   to serve

poppy seed *onion rings*

Serves 2

Oil to deep-fry
²/₃ cup (150 mL) all-purpose
  flour
2 Tbsp (25 mL) poppy seeds
1 Tbsp (15 mL) white mustard
  seeds
Salt and black pepper
2 large onions, cut into
  ¹/₂-in (1-cm) slices
A little milk

I don't always feel like making a batter when I fancy some onion rings, so this crisp flour coating makes an ideal alternative. The poppy and mustard seeds provide a good contrast to the soft texture of the onion.

Preparation time: 10 minutes Cooking time: 15 minutes

Heat the oil to 350°F (180°C) in a large pot or a deep-fryer.

Mix together all the dry ingredients. Separate the onion slices into rings.

Dip the rings into a little milk, then toss them in the spiced flour. Prepare the rings in about 3 batches, just before frying them.

Carefully lower the onion rings, a few at a time, into the hot oil. Fry for 3 to 4 minutes until golden brown, then scoop them out with a slotted spoon and drain on crumpled paper towels. Repeat until all the rings are fried.

Serve as a side dish, or on a bed of salad leaves as a quick snack.

spiced *onion balls*

Makes about 24

Oil to deep-fry
1¹/₄ cups (300 mL) fine whole
  wheat flour
1 tsp (5 mL) salt
¹/₂ tsp (2 mL) baking soda
1 Tbsp (15 mL) ground rice
1 Tbsp (15 mL) mild curry
  powder
1 tsp (2 mL) chili powder
1 small green chile, seeded and
  chopped fine
2 large onions, sliced fine
1 cup (250 mL) water

These fried onion balls are best made with very fine besan or chickpea flour, but I am using a very fine whole wheat flour, the type that is fine enough for pastry, which is more widely available. Don't make them too big, or they will not cook through in the center before burning.

Preparation time: 10 minutes Cooking time: about 20 minutes

Heat the oil in a deep-fryer to 330°F (170°C).

Mix all the dry ingredients together in a bowl, then add the chili powder, chopped green chile, and onions. Add more onion if necessary; there should be more onion than spiced flour.

Gradually add sufficient water to obtain a soft, thick paste.

Carefully lower heaped teaspoonfuls of mixture into the hot oil and fry for about 10 minutes, until browned and crisp.

Drain thoroughly on paper towels and serve with chutney or onion, radish, or cucumber raita (see page 50).

onion rings *in beer-batter*

A delicious batter for the ever-popular fried onion rings. Beer gives the batter an excellent flavor, and the addition of egg white keeps it crisp and light.

Preparation time: 15 minutes Cooking time: 10 minutes

Heat the oil to 375°F (190°C) in a large pan or a deep-fryer.

Blend the flour with the oil and beer in a bowl. Whisk the egg white until stiff, then fold it into the batter just before using – this is easiest with a wire whisk.

Separate the onion slices into rings. Coat them in the batter just before frying, then lower them carefully into the hot oil. Fry the rings for 3 to 4 minutes until golden brown, turning them over as necessary.

Remove the rings from the oil with a slotted spoon and drain them on crumpled paper towels. Continue cooking in batches.

Serve with steaks, broiled fish, or as a simple snack on their own with a garlic or tomato dip.

Serves 2

Oil to deep-fry

¾ cup (170 mL) all-purpose flour

3 Tbsp (45 mL) corn or vegetable oil

1 cup (250 mL) beer

1 large egg white

2 large red onions, cut into ½-inch (1-cm) slices

scallion *spring rolls*

Serves 4

3 cups (700 mL) prepared
   mixed stir-fry vegetables

6 scallions, cut into 2-in
   (5-cm) pieces then sliced fine
   lengthwise

8 or 16 sheets phyllo pastry,
   according to size

Peanut oil to brush

Oil to deep-fry

Chili dipping sauce to serve

These spring rolls with extra onion are very easy to prepare if you use a package of prepared stir-fry vegetables. Fry or bake according to your conscience – frying will produce a crisper result.

Preparation time: 20 minutes Cooking time: about 12 minutes

Mix the prepared stir-fry vegetables with the scallions. Preheat the oven to 425°F (220°C) if you are going to bake the rolls.

Prepare the phyllo pastry – you need 8 stacks of 6-in (15-cm) squares of phyllo, 4 sheets thick. Brush each sheet with oil before stacking.

Divide the vegetables among the pastry. Fold the bases up over the filling and fold in the sides, then roll up, sealing the edges firmly. It is very important to seal the edges if you are going to fry the rolls, otherwise they will unwrap and the filling will ooze out. A dab of water will "glue" the pastry.

Bake the rolls for 10 to 12 minutes in a hot oven, or deep-fry them 4 at a time in hot oil at 375°F (190°C) for 3 to 4 minutes, until golden brown. Turn carefully once during cooking. Drain the fried rolls well on plenty of crumpled paper towels.

Serve with a small salad or Asian herb garnish and plenty of chili dipping sauce.

onion, rosemary, *and gorgonzola crostini*

Serves 4

1 large shallot

16 prepared cocktail toast
   squares

4 scallions, chopped fine

1 Tbsp (15 mL) chopped fresh
   rosemary

2 sun-dried tomatoes, chopped
   fine

1 cup (250 mL) crumbled
   Gorgonzola

Salt and black pepper

A crispy hors d'oeuvre to serve with drinks. I rub the prepared toasts with the cut surface of a shallot for extra onion flavor. Using prepared cocktail toasts cuts down on preparation time.

Preparation time: 15 minutes Cooking time: 5 minutes

Cut the shallot in half and rub the surface over the toasts, then finely chop the shallot and place it in a bowl with the remaining ingredients. Mix well.

Preheat the broiler. Divide the topping among the flavored toasts, then broil them until the cheese is just starting to melt and brown. Serve immediately.

tomato *and scallion bruschettas*

These toasts have a scent of the Mediterranean about them, and the scallions used here make a welcome change from the more typical garlic. Add mozzarella cheese if you wish, to make a more substantial snack.

Preparation time: 30 minutes Cooking time: 10 minutes

Serves 2

Slice the tomatoes and place them in a bowl with the scallions. Season well, then add the oil and leave for 20 minutes, stirring from time to time.

Toast one side of the bread under a broiler, then turn it over and pile on the tomatoes and scallions. Reserve the olive oil. Broil until the tomatoes start to blacken – make sure all the bread is covered or it will burn.

Spoon the oil over the *bruschettas* and garnish with a small lettuce leaf or other greens to serve.

2 to 3 ripe plum tomatoes
2 scallions, sliced fine
Salt and black pepper
2 Tbsp (25 mL) olive oil
4 to 6 slices French bread, or
  2 slices whole wheat bread

cheese *and onion beignets*

Oil to deep-fry
4 Tbsp (50 mL) butter
⅔ cup (150 mL) water
½ cup (125 mL) all-purpose
  flour
2 medium eggs, beaten
½ cup (125 mL) grated Cheddar
  cheese
1 shallot, minced
Salt and cayenne pepper

These fried pastry puffs are really easy to make, but it is important to measure the ingredients accurately. Add the egg to the dough gradually – you may not need it all – you want the dough to hold its shape, so keep it quite stiff.

Preparation time: 15 minutes Cooking time: 10-12 minutes

Preheat the oil in a deep-fryer to 400°F (200°C).

To make the choux pastry, heat the butter and water together in a saucepan until the butter has melted, then bring to a rolling boil. Add the flour all at once – I usually sieve it onto a piece of wax paper to make it easier to tip into the pan. Immediately take the pan off the heat and beat vigorously, until the mixture forms a ball and leaves the sides of the pan. A sturdy wooden spoon works best.

Gradually add the beaten eggs, beating well between each addition, until they are well mixed into the dough, then add the cheese, shallot, and seasoning.

Carefully drop teaspoonfuls of the choux pastry into the hot fat and deep-fry for 3 to 4 minutes, until golden brown. Drain thoroughly on plenty of crumpled paper towels and serve hot.

roasted onion *and eggplant pâté*

1 large onion
1 medium eggplant
Salt and black pepper
Olive oil
1 cup (250 mL) cream cheese
1 clove garlic
Pinch chili powder
Lemon or lime juice to taste

This makes an excellent dip or spread, alternatively try it folded in tortillas.

Preparation time: 15 minutes Cooking time: 45 minutes, plus cooling time

Preheat the oven to 425°F (220°C).

Cut the onion into quarters and place on a baking sheet with the eggplant. Season lightly, then drizzle with olive oil. Roast in the hot oven for 45 minutes, until the eggplant is blackened and the skin wrinkled. Allow to cool.

Cut off and discard the end of the eggplant. Place the eggplant in the food processor with the onion, cream cheese, garlic, and chili powder and blend until completely smooth.

Season the pâté with salt and pepper and lemon or lime juice to taste.

cheese and onion beignets

onion *and chicken satay skewers*

Probably one of the best foods for barbecue! Soak the bamboo sticks in water to stop them scorching during cooking. This is also delicious made from finely sliced pork tenderloin.

Serves 4

Small piece ginger root
2 shallots, chopped
2 stalks lemongrass, bruised
  and chopped fine
2 Tbsp (25 mL) satay (peanut)
  sauce
1 tsp (5 mL) ground turmeric
1 Tbsp (15 mL) demerara sugar
½ tsp (2 mL) salt
Water
1 lb (450 g) chicken breast
  fillets or pork tenderloin,
  trimmed and sliced very fine

Preparation time: 15 minutes, plus 2 hours marinating Cooking time: about 10 minutes

Grate the ginger, gather up the pieces in your hand, then squeeze the juice into a small blender or jug. Add the shallots, lemongrass, satay sauce, turmeric, sugar, and salt. Blend until smooth, adding a little water if necessary.

Shred the chicken or pork, then marinate in the sauce in a small bowl for 2 hours. Turn the meat in the sauce once or twice.

Soak 16 wooden skewers in cold water for 30 minutes while the meat is marinating.

Thread the strips onto the skewers – do not pack too tightly, so the meat can cook through quickly.

Cook the skewers for 3 to 4 minutes on each side, either over a medium-hot barbecue or under a broiler. The cooking time will depend on the thickness of the meat. Serve hot, with a cucumber and chile salad.

soups, appetizers,

and hors d'oeuvres

salads

Stir-fried in cinnamon, chopped into cracked wheat or dressings, or teamed with hot duck or pickled herrings, onions and salads are perfect partners, with the versatile bulbs adding flavor, bite, and freshness.

onion *raita*

Serves 4

1 onion, sliced fine

2 Tbsp (25 mL) vegetable oil

1 tsp (5 mL) cumin seeds

1 red onion, sliced fine

1 small red chile, seeded and
   chopped fine (optional)

2–3 Tbsp (25–45 mL) chopped
   cilantro

1½ cups (350 mL) plain yogurt

Salt and black pepper

A refreshing salad to serve with fried dishes, or with plain-cooked steak.

It is also a cooling accompaniment to many Indian dishes.

Preparation time: 5 minutes Cooking time: 5 minutes

Cook the onion in the oil for about 3 to 4 minutes until softened but not browned. Add the cumin seeds and cook for a further 2 to 3 minutes until golden brown. Turn into a serving bowl.

Add all the remaining ingredients, seasoning well to taste. Allow to stand for 10 to 15 minutes before serving, if possible, to allow the flavors to blend.

salads

onion *caponata*

Caponata is generally thought of as an eggplant-based dish,

but here it is made extra special by the addition of onions.

Preparation time: 45 minutes Cooking time: 30 minutes

Layer the diced eggplant in a colander with salt, then allow to stand for 30 minutes. Rinse thoroughly in cold water, shake well, and pat dry on paper towels.

Pour most of the oil into a large skillet, add the eggplant and cook until browned and soft, which will take 10 to 12 minutes. In a separate pan, cook the onions, pickles, capers, and olives slowly in the remaining oil over very low heat for about 10 minutes, until softened. Add the sugar and vinegar and continue to cook slowly until the smell of the vinegar has gone.

Drain any excess oil from the eggplant, then add it to the other vegetables with the pine nuts. Add a little salt to season, if necessary. Serve the *caponata* warm or cold.

Serves 4

2 large eggplants, trimmed and
   cut into ½-in (1.25-cm) dice
Salt
½ cup (125 mL) light olive oil
2 red onions, sliced
1½ cups (350 mL) mixed pickled
   vegetables (onions, gherkins,
   pickled peppers, etc.), chopped
⅓ cup (80 mL) capers
½ cup (125 mL) pitted green
   olives
1 Tbsp (15 mL) sugar
⅔ cup (150 mL) red wine
   vinegar
2 Tbsp (25 mL) pine nuts

spiced beef *and onion salad*

Serves 2

3 Tbsp chile or peanut oil

6 oz (175 g) lean boneless beef, sliced thin, then cut into ³/₄-in (2-cm) strips

3 small heads bok choy, sliced thick

1 large carrot, julienned

6 scallions, cut into 1¹/₂-in (4-cm) pieces

1 Tbsp (15 mL) pickled ginger, chopped

1 tsp (5 ml) hot fresh chili paste

Soy sauce and salt to taste

Salad leaves to serve

Wafer-thin strips of beef for stir-fries make this a very quick salad to prepare – but tastes as if you have spent hours in the kitchen.

Preparation time: 10 minutes Cooking time: about 5 minutes

Heat a wok, add the oil, then stir-fry the beef for 1 to 2 minutes. Add the stalks of the bok choy with the carrot and scallions and stir-fry for a further 2 minutes.

Add the pickled ginger and chili paste with the bok choy leaves and cook for a further 1 minute.

Season the stir-fry with soy sauce and salt to taste, then spoon over a bed of salad leaves with all the pan juices and serve immediately.

onion *coleslaw*

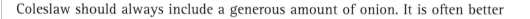

Serves 6

¹/₂ small green cabbage, shredded

3 large carrots, peeled and grated

1 red onion, chopped fine

4 scallions, trimmed and sliced fine

Salt and black pepper

¹/₂ cup (125 mL) mayonnaise

¹/₃ cup (80 mL) plain yogurt

Coleslaw should always include a generous amount of onion. It is often better the day after it is made, when the flavors have had a chance to blend.

Preparation time: 15 minutes

Mix all the vegetables together in a large bowl and season well.

Add the mayonnaise and yogurt and mix thoroughly, ensuring that all the vegetables are well coated in the dressing.

onion *and chile tabbouleh*

Tabbouleh, a salad of bulghur wheat, is usually flavored with herbs. In this version I use onions and chiles for a little more spice.

Serves 6

1 cup (250 mL) fine bulgur
2 cups (450 mL) boiling water
6 scallions, chopped fine
1 red and 1 green chile, chopped fine
1/2 cucumber, diced fine
1 cup (250 mL) chopped watercress
Juice of 1/2 lemon
Salt and black pepper
4 Tbsp (50 mL) green olive oil

Preparation time: 40 minutes

Place the bulgur in a bowl, pour over the boiling water, and allow to stand for 30 minutes. Drain, then squeeze dry through a fine sieve or in a clean dish towel.

Turn the bulgur into a large bowl and mix in all the remaining ingredients. Mix well, then serve at room temperature.

shallot caesar *salad*

Serves 2 as a main course or 4 as an appetizer

8 Tbsp (100 mL) freshly grated
    Parmesan cheese shavings
2 heads Boston lettuce, rinsed
    and broken into bite-size
    pieces
1 large banana shallot or
    2 regular ones, chopped fine
2 Tbsp (25 mL) olive oil
2 large eggs, beaten
2–3 Tbsp (25–45 mL) heavy
    cream
Salt and black pepper

For days when you can't live without a Caesar salad but your friend doesn't want garlic! Use the best Parmesan cheese you can find.

Preparation time: 5 minutes Cooking time: 15 minutes

Heat a large nonstick skillet, then carefully fry the cheese in 8 little mounds for $1\frac{1}{2}$ to 2 minutes, until golden brown and melted together into a crisp. Turn with a spatula and cook the other side. Cool on a wire rack.

Arrange the lettuce in a large bowl.

Cook the chopped shallot in the oil in a pot until softened but not browned. Beat the eggs with the cream and add to the pot. Cook gently until just starting to set.

Break up the Parmesan and add the crisp pieces to the lettuce with plenty of salt and pepper, then pour the egg dressing over. Mix thoroughly and serve immediately.

meat and fish main courses

The richness of slow-braised onions blends perfectly with red meat casseroles, while quick-fried or even raw onions can season fish and poultry dishes without dominating. Whether supporting or leading the flavors, the onion is fundamental.

beef *and onion turnovers*

12 oz (350 g) best stewing
  steak, chuck or blade, cubed
1 cup (250 mL) diced peeled
  potato
1 medium onion, chopped fine
Salt and black pepper
3 cups (700 mL) all-purpose
  flour, sifted
6 Tbsp (75 mL) butter or
  margarine
Cold water to mix

A traditional dish in Cornwall, England – meat and

vegetables held in a pastry sandwich.

Preparation time: 45 minutes Cooking time: 1¼ hours

Preheat the oven to 425°F (220°C). Lightly oil a baking sheet.

Cut the stewing steak into ¼-in (6-mm) dice, then mix it with the vegetables and season well.

Mix the flour with a good pinch of salt, then cut in the butter until the mixture resembles fine bread crumbs. Add just enough cold water to bind the dough, then divide in four. On a lightly floured board roll out each piece into an 8-in (20-cm) circle – use a plate to cut around.

Divide the filling among the pastry circles, then dampen the edges and bring them together over the filling. Seal them together, then flute the edges decoratively with your fingers. Place on the oiled baking sheet.

Bake the turnovers for 15 minutes, then reduce the temperature to 325°F (170°C) for a further 1 hour. Serve the turnovers hot or cold – they are great picnic food.

poached smoked haddock *with sweet onion cream sauce*

Serves 4

2 large sweet onions, sliced
  thin
2 Tbsp (25 mL) olive oil
4 pieces smoked haddock, each
  weighing about 6 oz (175 g)
⅔ cup (150 mL) vegetable or
  fish broth
3 Tbsp (45 mL) heavy cream
Salt and black pepper
1–2 Tbsp (15–25 mL) chopped
  fresh chives

Onions and fish aren't always perfect partners, but sweet onions complement

the subtle flavor of fish very well.

Preparation time: 10 minutes Cooking time: 20 minutes

Cook the onions in the oil for 5 to 8 minutes until softened and a rich golden brown.

Place the haddock on top of the onions, add the broth, then cover and simmer slowly for 5 minutes, or until the fish is just done.

Carefully lift the fish from the pan and set aside. Remove the onions with a slotted spoon and make nests of them on each of four warmed plates. Arrange the fish on top and keep warm.

Boil the onion juices until well reduced then stir in the cream. Season the sauce to taste then add the chives. Spoon the sauce over the fish and serve immediately.

beef and onion turnovers

sausage, onion, *and egg pie*

A comforting winter dish – leftover cooked ham could

be used instead of sausages if you wish.

Serves 6 to 8

2 large onions, cut into 4 or 6
1 cup (250 mL) water
¹/₂ tsp (2 mL) ground mace or
   2 bay leaves
1 cup (250 mL) milk
3 Tbsp (45 mL) butter
2 Tbsp (25 mL) flour
Salt and black pepper to taste
6 to 8 thick sausages, cut into
   1¹/₂-in (4-cm) chunks
4 hard-cooked eggs, quartered
2 Tbsp (25 mL) capers
   (optional)

PASTRY
1²/₃ cups (400 mL) all-purpose
   flour
Pinch salt
2 Tbsp (25 mL) butter

Preparation time: 45 minutes Cooking time: 45 minutes

Place the onions in a saucepan with the water and mace or bay leaves. Cover and simmer until tender, about 15 minutes. Remove the flavorings and add the milk, butter, and flour. Bring to a boil, stirring continuously until thickened. Season to taste then remove from heat and allow to cool slightly.

Preheat the oven to 400°F (200°C). Brown the sausages on all sides in a nonstick skillet. Combine the sauce with the sausages, eggs, and capers (if using), then turn into a buttered pie dish.

Mix the flour and salt, then cut in the butter until the mixture resembles fine bread crumbs. Add sufficient water to bind to a stiff dough, then roll out on a lightly floured board and use to cover the pie. Make a hole in the middle of the pastry with a knife to allow the steam to escape and to keep the pastry crisp, and use any trimmings to make pastry leaves to decorate the pie. Place the pie on a baking sheet, in case some of the filling bubbles over.

Bake in the hot oven for 45 minutes, or until the pastry is well browned. Serve immediately with freshly cooked vegetables in season.

chicken and *onion pot roast*

A celebration of onions in a simple dish. I love pot roasts, which are a meal in themselves, needing no other accompaniment than crusty bread.

Preparation time: 25 minutes Cooking time: about 1³/₄ hours

Cook the shallots in the oil in a heavy-bottomed pot that is just large enough to take the chicken. Cook until browned on all sides, then scoop them from the pot with a slotted spoon and set aside.

Add the whole chicken, brown quickly on all sides, then leave it in the pot, breast-side down. Press the quartered onions down the sides of the pot around it, with the thyme and lemon rind.

Season the chicken well, then add the broth with the saffron strands mixed in well. Bring to a boil and cover with a tight-fitting lid. Reduce the heat and simmer very gently for 45 minutes.

Turn the chicken over, then nestle it back down among the onions. Add the shallots and cook slowly, covered, for a further 45 minutes, or until the chicken is done – the juices should run clear from the thigh when pierced with a skewer.

Carefully draining any juices from the body cavity, transfer the chicken to a warm plate and leave it to rest for 10 minutes.

Add the scallions to the sauce and boil briefly to reduce the liquid. Season to taste.

Carve the chicken and serve with the onions and juices spooned over.

Serves 4 to 6

12 to 15 shallots, peeled but
  left whole
3 Tbsp (45 mL) olive oil
1 oven-ready chicken, about
  4 lb (1.8 kg)
2 large yellow onions and
  2 red onions, quartered
3 to 4 large sprigs thyme
4 large strips pared lemon rind
Salt and black pepper
1 cup (250 mL) chicken or
  vegetable broth
Few strands saffron
8 scallions, chopped fine

lamb and *onion curry*

Serves 6

2¼ lb (1 kg) onions, chopped

1½-in (4-cm) piece ginger root,
  peeled and chopped

6 cloves garlic

1 Tbsp (15 mL) black
  peppercorns

2 Tbsp (25 mL) coriander seeds

1 Tbsp (15 mL) cumin seeds

1 tsp (5 mL) green cardamom
  pods or ½ tsp (2 mL) ground
  cardamom

2 Tbsp (25 mL) oil

2¼ lb (1 kg) lean boneless
  lamb, cut into 1½-in (4-cm)
  cubes

2 tsp (10 mL) turmeric

3 dried red chiles

2 tsp (10 mL) salt

1 Tbsp (15 mL) vinegar of your
  choice

1 cup (250 mL) water

1 tsp (5 mL) garam masala

⅓ cup (80 mL) coconut cream

⅔ cup (150 mL) heavy cream

Cilantro to garnish

Onions are an essential part of a curry – I think they are best puréed to make a base for a rich, spicy sauce.

Preparation time: 30 minutes Cooking time: 1 hour 30 minutes

Purée the onions, ginger, and garlic into a smooth paste in a food processor.

Heat a large pan then add the peppercorns, coriander seeds, cumin seeds, and cardamom and cook for about 30 seconds until fragrant. Turn out of the pan into a mortar or a small bowl and allow to cool slightly.

Heat the oil in the pan, then add the lamb and cook until colored all over – it does not need to be really brown. Add the onion purée and cook for 4 to 5 minutes.

Crush the spices with a pestle or the end of a rolling pin then add them to the lamb with the turmeric and dried chiles. Cook for a further 2 to 3 minutes.

Stir in the salt, vinegar, and water, then bring to a gentle boil. Cover the pan and simmer slowly for 1 hour, until the lamb is just tender.

Stir in the garam masala, coconut cream, and cream and continue cooking, uncovered, for 30 minutes, until the lamb is meltingly soft and the sauce has thickened.

Season to taste and serve garnished with cilantro.

lamb and onion curry

mussels with *onions, apple, and cider*

Serves 2 as a main course or 4 as an appetizer

2¼ lb (1 kg) mussels

1 large onion, chopped fine or sliced

1 tsp (5 mL) ground mace

2 Tbsp (25 mL) olive oil

1 clove garlic, minced

1 tart green apple, such as Granny Smith, cored, and chopped fine

1 cup (250 mL) hard cider

2 bay leaves

Black pepper, sugar, and lemon juice to taste

2 Tbsp (25 mL) crème fraîche or sour cream

2 Tbsp (25 mL) chopped parsley

I have always loved mussels – there are so many ways of cooking them and this is my latest idea – the flavor is intense.

Preparation time: 15 minutes Cooking time: 10-12 minutes

Wash and scrub the mussels, discarding any which are damaged or which do not close when tapped sharply. Pull off any beards.

Cook the onion with the mace in the oil in a large pot until softened, then add the garlic and apple. Add the cider and bay leaves. Bring to a rapid boil.

Stir in the mussels, cover the pot, and cook over very high heat for about 3 minutes, shaking the pan occasionally, until the mussels have all opened. Discard any that have failed to do so. Spoon the mussels into warmed serving plates while the pan is still on the heat – this starts the sauce reducing quickly.

Continue to boil the liquor quickly until reduced by about half, then remove from the heat and season with pepper, sugar, and a squeeze of lemon juice. Discard the bay leaves, then whisk in the crème fraîche or sour cream and parsley.

Spoon the sauce over the mussels and serve immediately, with plenty of crusty bread to mop up the sauce.

liver *and onions*

Serves 4

2 large onions, sliced but not too fine

3 Tbsp (45 mL) olive oil

Salt and black pepper

1¼ lb (600 g) liver, sliced thin

2 Tbsp (25 mL) flour

1 tsp (5 mL) dry mustard powder

1 cup (250 mL) onion or vegetable broth

Chopped parsley to garnish

I love liver, but always choose lamb's or calf's liver which are milder than pig's. The best way to cook it is with lots of caramelized onions.

Preparation time: 10 minutes Cooking time: 15 minutes

Cook the onions in the olive oil in a large skillet for 4 to 5 minutes while preparing the liver. Season the thinly sliced liver.

Mix the flour and mustard powder together and generously dust the liver with it. Move the onions to one side in the skillet, add the liver, and fry for 3 to 4 minutes on medium-high heat on each side. Do not overcook, or the liver will be tough.

Transfer the liver to warmed plates, then add the broth to the pan. Bring to a boil, stirring all the time, and season the gravy to taste. Add a little more broth if you like a thinner sauce. Pour the onion gravy over the liver and garnish with plenty of chopped parsley before serving.

mussels with onions, apple, and cider

italian braised beef *with onion and eggplant*

Serves 4

2 Tbsp (25 mL) all-purpose
flour

Salt and freshly ground black
pepper

1 tsp (5 mL) mild chili powder

4 beef shanks, each weighing
about 6 oz (175 g)

5 Tbsp (65 mL) olive oil

2 large cloves garlic, sliced

2 Tbsp (25 mL) chopped fresh
oregano

14 fl oz (398 mL) canned
chopped tomatoes

2 cups (450 mL) beef or
vegetable broth

2 medium eggplants, cut into
chunks about 2-in (5-cm)

1 large onion, cut into 6

1 red onion, cut into 6

1 red bell pepper, seeded and
diced

1 clove garlic, chopped fine

8 slices pancetta or very thin
bacon

Chopped parsley to garnish

A perfect dinner or supper party dish – the meat cooks slowly in the oven until very tender. Serve with a simple vegetable stir-fry.

Preparation time: 15 minutes Cooking time: about 3½ hours

Preheat the oven to 325°F (170°C). Mix together the flour, seasonings, and chili powder on a plate. Trim the beef and turn it in the flour.

Heat 3 tablespoons (45 mL) of the oil in an ovenproof casserole, add the beef, and brown well on both sides. Stir in the garlic, oregano, and tomatoes and just enough broth to cover the meat. Bring to a boil then cover the pan and transfer to the oven for 3 hours, or until the beef is meltingly tender.

Heat the remaining oil in a hot wok, add the eggplant, and cook quickly to brown. Add the onion and cook for a further 3 minutes, then add the bell pepper and garlic and stir-fry for 2 minutes.

Remove the beef from the tomato sauce, transfer to a plate, cover with foil, and keep warm. Add the vegetables to the tomato sauce and simmer, uncovered, for about 10 minutes, until the vegetables are just done and the sauce is well reduced.

Dry-fry the pancetta or bacon in the wok until crisp.

To serve, make a mound of vegetables in the center of four warmed serving plates and top each with a piece of beef. Spoon the sauce over and around the plate, then garnish each helping with a little of the crisp pancetta or bacon and some chopped parsley. Serve immediately.

veal with onion *and tuna mayonnaise*

This is an elegant summer dish – perfect for relaxed entertaining because it has to be prepared a day in advance. Adding onion to the veal as it cooks and shallot to the mayonnaise lifts the flavor enormously.

Preparation time: 30 minutes Cooking time: 2 hours, plus overnight chilling

Trim the joint and open it out on a chopping board. Pound the anchovies, one of the chopped onions, and capers together, or process to a chunky paste with a hand blender. Add a little pepper, then smear the paste over the veal. Roll up the joint, tie it securely, and place in a pot just large enough to hold it.

Press the remaining chopped onions around the sides of the joint, add the peppercorns and parsley, then pour in the broth, adding just enough to cover the veal.

Bring to a boil, then half cover the pan and simmer very slowly for 2 hours, until the veal is just tender. Leave to cool in the broth.

Chill the veal well (if possible, I like to leave it overnight in the broth in the refrigerator). Slice to serve.

To make the mayonnaise, whip the tuna, the remaining anchovies, and the shallot with the tomato paste, lemon juice, and mayonnaise. Season to taste – you will probably only need pepper. Stir in the chopped parsley, then serve spooned over the veal slices.

Serves 6 to 8

2¼-lb (1.2-kg) joint boneless veal

6 anchovy fillets, chopped

3 onions, chopped fine

2 Tbsp (25 mL) capers, roughly
  chopped

Salt and black pepper

6 black peppercorns

4 large sprigs parsley

2¼ cups (500 mL) chicken or
  vegetable broth

MAYONNAISE

3½ oz (100 g) canned tuna,
  drained

6 anchovy fillets

1 shallot, chopped fine

1 Tbsp (15 mL) tomato paste

Juice of 1 lemon

1 cup (250 mL) mayonnaise

2 Tbsp (25 mL) chopped flat leaf
  parsley

pork with *caramelized onions and apples*

Serves 4

1 Tbsp (15 mL) butter

4 Tbsp (50 mL) olive oil

2 apples, each cut into 4 thick
slices

1 Tbsp (15 mL) sugar

1 sweet and 1 red onion, sliced
thick

1 lb (500 g) pork tenderloin,
trimmed and cut into ½-in
(1-cm) slices

1 Tbsp (15 mL) flour

Salt and black pepper

1 Tbsp (15 mL) coriander

²/₃ cup (150 mL) vegetable
broth

2 bay leaves

²/₃ cup (150 mL) heavy cream

Chopped chives to garnish

This is a classic combination of flavors – one which has endured for years simply because it is so good.

Preparation time: 15 minutes Cooking time: 15 minutes

Heat the butter and 2 tablespoons (25 mL) of oil together in a large skillet. Turn the apple slices in the sugar, then fry them quickly on both sides until browned. Transfer to a plate and reserve for garnish.

Add the onions to the juices in the skillet and toss them well – they will quickly start to brown and caramelize. Cook over moderate heat for about 5 minutes, stirring frequently. Turn onto a plate.

Heat the remaining oil in the pan. Dust the pork in the flour, seasonings, and coriander, then brown it quickly on both sides. Add the broth and bay leaves, bring to a boil, then simmer for 5 minutes.

Return the onions to the skillet with the cream and simmer for a further 5 minutes.

Season to taste with extra salt and pepper then serve garnished with the reserved apple rings and chopped chives.

spiced pork with onions, *chiles, and coconut*

Serves 4

2 Tbsp (25 mL) sunflower or
peanut oil

1 boneless leg of pork,
weighing about 2¼ lb (1 kg)

2 large onions, quartered

1 tsp (15 mL) turmeric

2 hot red chiles, chopped fine

2 tsp (10 mL) fresh tamarind
paste (optional)

3 to 4 lime leaves, chopped fine
or finely grated rind of
2 limes

2 cups (450 mL) milk

3 Tbsp (45 mL) coconut cream

Salt and black pepper

A pleasantly spiced oven pot roast with modern, fusion flavors.

A great dinner party dish.

Preparation time: 20 minutes Cooking time: 2½ hours

Preheat the oven to 325°F (170°C).

Heat the oil in an ovenproof casserole, then add the pork and brown quickly on all sides. Transfer the meat to a plate.

Add the onions, spices, and lime leaves or rind to the pot and cook until the onions are lightly browned. Gradually add the milk, scraping up any bits from the bottom of the pan, then bury the pork back in among the onions.

Bring just to a boil, cover, and place in the oven for 2 to 2½ hours, until the meat is tender. Remove the meat from the ovenproof casserole and allow to stand for 10 minutes before carving.

Whisk the coconut cream into the spiced onions and milk, season, and heat gently until ready to serve. Carve the pork, and serve with the onion and coconut sauce spooned over – broccoli and mashed potatoes or rice are good with this.

meat and fish

main courses

pork with caramelized onions and apples

eggplant, red onion, *and ground beef bake*

Serves 4

1 lb (500 g) lean ground beef

2 tsp (10 mL) ground cumin

1 Tbsp (15 mL) coriander

1 tsp (5 mL) ground ginger

14 fl oz (398 mL) canned
   chopped tomatoes

1 Tbsp (15 mL) chopped fresh
   oregano

2 bay leaves

Salt and black pepper

2 medium eggplants, sliced

²/₃ cup (150 mL) olive oil

1 large red onion, cut into
   thin rings

¹/₃ cup (80 mL) slivered almonds

1 large egg, beaten

1 cup (250 mL) milk

The mild red onion flavor is offset by the spicy ground beef filling – use lamb if you prefer. You can scatter grated cheese over the top and brown the dish instead of using almonds and the egg custard.

Preparation time: 40 minutes Cooking time: 1 hour

Preheat the oven to 400°F (200°C).

Cook the beef in a nonstick saucepan over high heat until the fat and juices start to run. Add the spices and continue to cook until the meat is well browned.

Add the tomatoes, oregano, bay leaves, and some seasoning, then leave to simmer for about 20 minutes, or until required. Season again to taste.

Fry the eggplant slices in two batches in a large skillet. They will absorb all the oil and try to demand more, but don't give in! Fry until lightly browned.

Arrange half the eggplant slices in the bottom of a buttered ovenproof dish, then pour on the beef. Cover with the remaining eggplant, pressing them down well into the browned beef.

Separate the onion into rings and arrange them over the eggplant. Cover with foil then bake in the preheated oven for 40 minutes.

Lower the oven temperature to 325°F (170°C). Remove the bake from the oven, take off the foil and scatter the almonds over the onions.

Beat the egg with the milk, add a little seasoning, then pour the mixture over the almonds. Return to the oven for a further 15 to 20 minutes, until the topping is set. Serve hot with freshly cooked vegetables in season.

duck breasts with *shallots and sherry*

This is a really simple recipe to prepare and cook, but it is impressive – and delicious.

Serves 4

2 banana or large shallots, chopped fine
4 duck breast fillets
Coarse sea salt
4 Tbsp (50 mL) sherry vinegar
4 Tbsp (50 mL) medium sherry

Preparation time: 5 minutes Cooking time: 40 minutes

Preheat the oven to 400°F (200°C).

Place the shallots in the bottom of a small roasting pan, then set the duck breasts, fat side uppermost, on a rack over them. Rub the breasts generously with coarse salt, then roast them in the hot oven for 30 to 35 minutes, until the juices run clear. Remove the rack and keep the duck warm for at least 5 minutes before carving.

Spoon off all but 2 tablespoons (25 mL) of the fat – keep it for roasting potatoes. Add the sherry vinegar to the pan and heat it gently on the stove, scraping up any bits from the bottom.

Stir in the sherry, bring to a boil, then season to taste.

Slice the duck breasts and serve with the sauce spooned over.

onion-studded lamb *with scallion mash*

Shoulder of lamb is by far my favorite roasting cut because the meat is so sweet and succulent. Instead of larding the joint with garlic or rosemary I like to use sliced shallots, which give a really good onion flavor.

Serve with Champ (scallion mash) – page 125.

Serves 6

2 banana shallots, or 4 to 5 button shallots, half chopped fine and half slivered
3 large sprigs thyme
1 large shoulder of lamb, weighing about 5 lb (2.3 kg)
Salt and black pepper
1 Tbsp (15 mL) flour
About 2 cups (450 mL) vegetable broth

Preparation time: 15 minutes Cooking time: about 2 hours, depending on size of joint

Preheat the oven to 400°F (200°C). Arrange the chopped shallots in the bottom of a roasting pan and top with the thyme.

Pierce the lamb repeatedly with the tip of a sharp knife, then insert slivers of the shallot. The more patience you have to persist with this, the better the flavor will be.

Place the lamb on top of the shallots in the roasting pan, season generously, then rub the seasonings into the fat.

Roast the lamb for 1½ to 1¾ hours, then allow to stand for 15 minutes before carving. Discard the thyme, but use the chopped shallots and pan juices to make gravy by adding the flour and stirring over low heat until bubbling. Gradually add in the broth, then bring to a boil, stirring all the time. Season to taste, simmer for 1 to 2 minutes, then serve with the sliced lamb and Champ.

venison and *onion pie*

Venison makes an ideal filling for this traditional raised pie as it hardly shrinks at all during cooking. A generous amount of onion in the pie adds lots of flavor and keeps the meat moist.

Serves 6 to 8

1¾ lb (750 g) stewing venison, or boneless pork loin, diced
1 lb (500 g) onions, chopped
Salt and black pepper
6 juniper berries, crushed
3 Tbsp (45 mL) red wine
2 Tbsp (25 mL) olive oil
1 egg, beaten
1 tsp (5 mL) gelatin
⅔ cup (150 mL) boiling vegetable broth

PASTRY

2 cups (450 mL) all-purpose flour
1 tsp (5 mL) salt
¾ cup (175 mL) shortening
½ cup (125 mL) water and milk, mixed

Preparation time: 45 minutes Cooking time: 1½-1¾ hours

Prepare the pastry. Place the flour and salt in a bowl and make a well in the center. Chop the shortening, add it to the liquids, then heat until melted. Bring to a rolling boil, then pour into the flour and mix immediately into a soft, manageable dough. Knead until smooth on a lightly floured surface, then cover and leave to cool slightly.

Preheat the oven to 425°F (220°C). Process the venison and onions in a food processor or meat grinder until chopped fine, then season well. Add the juniper berries and moisten the meat with the wine and oil.

Roll out two-thirds of the pastry and use to line an 8-in (20-cm) deep springform pan. Pack the meat into the pie, then roll out the remaining pastry to make a lid. Moisten the edges of the pastry, then seal the top and sides together, pressing the edge into a decorative crust. Make a small slit in the center of the lid and use any pastry trimmings to make decorative leaves.

Brush the top of the pie with egg, then bake in the hot oven for 15 minutes. Lower the temperature to 350°F (180°C) and cook for a further 1 hour.

Carefully loosen and remove the sides of the pan trying not to break the pastry, then brush all the pastry again with beaten egg. Continue to cook for a further 20 to 30 minutes, brushing with egg once or twice more until the pastry is a dark, golden brown. Remove the pie and leave to cool slightly.

Dissolve the gelatin in the hot broth then pour it carefully into the pie – you will probably only get a small amount in as the meat hardly shrinks at all during cooking. Leave the pie until cold, then chill it for 2 to 3 hours before slicing. Serve cold, with some strong pickles and a green salad.

venison and onion pie

chinese baked salmon *with scallions and ginger*

Serves 4 to 6

1 small whole salmon, or a
　　large piece of salmon,
　　weighing about 2¾ lb
　　(1.2 kg)
8 scallions, trimmed and sliced
　　fine
2-in (5-cm) piece ginger root,
　　peeled and chopped fine
1 to 2 red chiles, seeded and
　　chopped fine
Light soy sauce
¼ cup (50 mL) sesame oil

The Chinese usually serve a whole fish at their New Year's banquets. I like this at any time of the year – the spicing adds extra flavor to the salmon.

Preparation time: 15 minutes Cooking time: 35 minutes

Preheat the oven to 425°F (220°C). Lightly oil a large sheet of heavy foil, big enough to enclose the salmon, and place it on a lipped baking sheet.

Trim the salmon and slash the flesh deeply three times on each side – this helps the fish to cook more quickly. Place the fish on the foil and insert half the scallions, all the ginger, and the chiles into the cavity – press a little of the onion mixture into the slits as well, if you like. Shake just a little soy sauce over the fish, then wrap it loosely in the foil. Bake in the hot oven for about 30 minutes, until the flesh offers no resistance when pierced with the tip of a sharp knife. Take care not to overcook the salmon or it will be dry.

Divide the salmon into portions and scatter the remaining scallions among them. Meanwhile, heat the sesame oil in a small pan, then pour it over the salmon just before serving.

homemade beef burgers *with scallions*

Serves 4

1 lb (500 g) ground beef
1 cup (250 mL) coarsely grated
　　mozzarella cheese
4 scallions, trimmed and
　　chopped very fine
Salt and black pepper
1 egg yolk
Rolls or baps and salad to serve

Homemade beef burgers are a real treat. Adding onion gives them loads of flavor, but make sure it is chopped fine or the burgers may fall apart during cooking.

Preparation time: 15 minutes Cooking time: 12 minutes

Mix all the ingredients together in a bowl, binding them with the egg yolk. Shape into four burgers – wetting your hands makes them easier to handle.

Heat a ridged grill pan until hot. Add the burgers and cook over moderate heat for 4 to 5 minutes on each side. No additional oil should be necessary – just rely on the fat in the meat. Serve hot in baps or burger rolls with salad.

chinese baked salmon with scallions and ginger

traditional steak and *onion pudding*

Serves 6 to 8

2 large onions, sliced very thin

1³/₄ lb (750 g) best braising
  steak, cut into ³/₄-in (2-cm)
  cubes

2 cups (150 mL) mushrooms,
  sliced thick

Salt and black pepper

4 cups (900 mL) flour

1 Tbsp (15 mL) baking powder

1 tsp (5 mL) salt

2¹/₂ cups (600 mL) lard or
  margarine

Cold water to mix

²/₃ cup (150 mL) beer

A variation of the classic English meat pudding – a good helping of onions provides a tasty alternative to the traditional pairing of steak and kidney.

Preparation time: 40 minutes Cooking time: 4-5 hours

Half-fill the bottom of a steamer with water and bring to a boil. Lightly butter a 2¹/₄-quart (2-L) pudding dish.

Mix together the onions, steak, mushrooms, and seasoning.

Sift the flour and baking powder together into a large bowl, add the salt, and stir in the lard or margarine. Mix to a soft manageable dough with cold water, then knead lightly on a floured surface.

Roll the pastry out into a large circle, about twice the diameter of the pudding dish rim. Cut away a segment (about one-third) of the dough, then press the remainder into the basin to line the base and sides, sealing any joins with a little water.

Pack the meat into the pudding, then pour in the beer. Roll out the remaining pastry to form a lid and use it to cover the pudding, damping and sealing the edges together. Make a small slit in the lid. It is no problem if the pudding does not completely fill the basin.

Cover with greased parchment paper and foil, making a fold in the covers to allow for the pastry to rise. Tie securely, to keep the cover on and the steam out.

Steam the pudding over boiling water for 4 to 5 hours – the longer the better. Top up the water as required. Add a little boiling broth or vegetable water to the meat when serving – cut away the first portion of pastry from the lid, then pour the extra liquid into the pudding. Serve with a selection of freshly cooked vegetables.

braised pheasant *with onions and celery*

Braised in a sauce that is sweet, sour, and fruity, the pheasant may be cooked quickly to keep the vegetables crisp, or slowly, to provide a more meltingly tender result. Time and preference will dictate.

Preparation time: 45 minutes Cooking time: 1 hour, or 1¹⁄₂–1³⁄₄ hours

Preheat the oven to 400°F (200°C). Dust the pheasants generously with the flour, season then brown the portions well in the oil in a large skillet.

Meanwhile, place the prepared vegetables and cranberries in a casserole dish that will take the pheasants in one layer, and bury the thyme in the vegetables. Nestle the pheasants into the vegetables.

Add all the remaining ingredients to the pan and bring to a boil. Pour over the pheasants, then cover with a lid or foil.

Cook in the hot oven for 10 minutes, then lower the temperature to 375°F (190°C) for 45 to 50 minutes, or to 325°F (160°C) for 1¹⁄₂ to 1³⁄₄ hours. The pheasant is cooked if the juices run clear when the thigh is pierced with the tip of a sharp knife.

Season the sauce to taste, then serve the pheasant on a bed of the vegetables with the juices spooned over and garnished with celery leaves. Mashed potatoes is a good accompaniment.

Serves 4

2 hen pheasants, cut
  lengthwise in half
2 Tbsp (25 mL) flour
Salt and black pepper
4 Tbsp (50 mL) olive oil
6 stalks celery, trimmed and cut
  into 2-in (5-cm) pieces
  (reserve the leaves to garnish)
2 large onions, cut into 6
2 large carrots, cut into 1-in
  (2.5-cm) pieces
¹⁄₃ cup (80 mL) dried cranberries
4–5 large sprigs thyme
Juice of 1 lemon
3 Tbsp (45 mL) red wine vinegar
¹⁄₄ cup (50 mL) clear honey
1 cup (250 mL) chicken or
  vegetable broth

pasta with onions, *clams, and tomato*

Serves 2

1 onion, chopped fine

1 Tbsp (15 mL) olive oil

²/₃ cup (150 mL) fish broth,
dry white wine, or a mixture
of both

1 clove garlic, minced

2 Tbsp (25 mL) chopped,
fresh mixed herbs for fish
(dill, chervil, flat leaf parsley)

1 lb (500 g) clams, rinsed and
scrubbed if necessary

2 cups (225 mL) pasta,
freshly cooked

Salt and black pepper

2 tomatoes, seeded and
chopped

Chopped parsley to garnish

A perfect supper dish – plenty of flavor, interesting textures,

colorful to look at, and quick to prepare.

Preparation time: 10 minutes Cooking time: 12-15 minutes

Cook the onion slowly in the oil until soft and translucent. Add the liquid and bring to a rapid boil, then add the garlic, herbs, and clams. Cover and cook for 3 to 4 minutes, until the clams have just opened. Discard any clams that do not open. Shake the pan from time to time.

Drain the pasta, then add the clams and onions to the pasta along with a piece of butter and some seasoning. Toss together.

Meanwhile, boil the onion and clam juices with the chopped tomatoes for 2 minutes, then pour over the pasta. Mix well and serve immediately, garnished with chopped parsley.

sausages and onions *with beer gravy*

Serves 2

2 Tbsp (25 mL) olive oil

6 thick sausages

2 large onions, sliced thin

1 Tbsp (15 mL) flour

²/₃ cup (150 mL) beer

²/₃ cup (150 mL) onion or
vegetable broth or water

Salt and black pepper

Mashed potatoes to serve

A new twist on a traditional English favorite. Accompanied by a helping of

mashed potatoes is a great way to serve these sausages.

Preparation time: 10 minutes Cooking time: 35 minutes

Heat the oil in a large skillet then add the sausages and brown them quickly on all sides to seal them.

Stir in the onions, toss in the hot oil, then lower the heat to medium and cook for 20 minutes, turning the sausages occasionally.

Remove the sausages from the skillet and keep them warm. Scatter the flour over the onions, then stir it in over the heat obliterating any lumps that form immediately. Gradually add the beer and broth, then bring the gravy to a boil, stirring continuously.

Season to taste. I like to serve this with a mound of mashed potatoes, the sausages resting against it, then the gravy spooned around the plate and vegetables scattered among the onions.

pasta with onions, clams, and tomato

teriyaki venison with *onion and sour cherries*

Serves 4

4 venison steaks, about
  6 oz (175 g) each
Salt and black pepper
Generous pinch dried
  crushed chiles
2 Tbsp (25 mL) peanut oil
$^3/_4$ cup (175 mL) plus 3 Tbsp
  (40 mL) bottled teriyaki
  marinade
$^1/_3$ cup (80 mL) dried sour
  cherries
$^2/_3$ cup (150 mL) vegetable or
  chicken broth
1 small sweet onion, chopped
  fine
1 Tbsp (15 mL) peanut oil
Black pepper and sugar to taste
Cilantro to garnish

The sweetness of the onion combines well with the salty teriyaki marinade

and flavorful sour cherries in this delicious dinner party dish.

If dried cherries are unavailable, substitute dried cranberries.

Preparation time: 25 minutes, plus marinating time Cooking time: 12–15 minutes

Season the steaks lightly, and place them in a strong, resealable plastic bag. Add the chiles, oil, and 3 tablespoons (45 mL) of the teriyaki marinade, then expel the air from the bag and seal it firmly. Rub the marinade thoroughly into the meat, then leave in the fridge for at least 2 hours.

Soak the cherries in the broth while the venison is marinating.

Carefully remove the steaks from the bag and reserve the marinade. Pat the meat dry on paper towels. Heat a ridged grill pan, add the steaks, and cook for 3 to 4 minutes on each side, depending on thickness and how rare you like your meat.

Meanwhile, cook the onion in the oil in a small pan until soft, then add the remaining bottled teriyaki, the cherries and some of their soaking broth, and the reserved marinade. Bring to a boil then simmer for 5 minutes. Season to taste and add a little more broth if necessary.

Serve the steaks sliced with the sauce spooned over, garnished with cilantro. This is great served with Champ (page 125).

teriyaki venison with onion and sour cherries

spanish-style cod *with onion and bell peppers*

Serves 4

1 lb (500 g) cod fillet or similar white fish, such as haddock, skinned

3 Tbsp (45 mL) olive oil

1 large red onion, sliced fine

1 cup (250 mL) sliced button mushrooms

1 red and 1 green bell pepper, seeded and sliced

Salt and white pepper

½ cup (125 mL) white wine vinegar

½ cup (125 mL) water

1 Tbsp (15 mL) sugar

Onions give lots of flavor to this traditional dish of lightly cooked cod – a great summer dish.

Preparation time: 15 minutes Cooking time: 15 minutes, plus 24 hours chilling time

Cut the fish into bite-size pieces. Heat 2 tablespoons (30 mL) of the oil in a large skillet and fry the fish until just done, then transfer it to a glass or ceramic dish.

Heat the remaining oil in the skillet, add the onion, and cook until soft but not browned. Stir in the mushrooms and peppers and cook for a further 1 to 2 minutes – the vegetables should remain crisp.

Spoon the vegetables over the fish and season lightly with salt and pepper.

Pour the vinegar and water into the skillet and bring to a boil. Add the sugar, stir until dissolved, then pour over the fish and vegetables. Allow to cool then cover and refrigerate for 24 hours. Serve with crusty olive bread.

spanish-style cod with onion and bell peppers

chicken, onion, *and bean sprout risotto*

Serves 4

2 large onions, sliced fine

2 Tbsp (25 mL) olive oil

2 chicken breast fillets, sliced

1 red bell pepper, seeded and sliced

3 cups (700 mL) cracked wheat or kamut

2¼ cups (500 mL) vegetable or chicken broth

3 Tbsp (45 mL) tamari or soy sauce

2 handfuls bean sprouts

1 cup (250 mL) dry-roasted, unsalted peanuts

Salt and black pepper

Chopped parsley to garnish

I love risottos made with cracked wheat – they have more crunch than those made with rice. Here the onions and chicken really star for flavor, along with the peanuts.

Preparation time: 15 minutes Cooking time: 25 minutes

Cook the onions in the oil in a large skillet until soft and just starting to brown, add the chicken, and stir-fry until it is white all over.

Add the bell pepper and cracked wheat, and toss them in the pan juices, then add the broth. Season with the tamari or soy sauce, bring to a boil, and simmer gently for 15 minutes, until most of the broth has been absorbed.

Add the bean sprouts and peanuts. Season with salt and pepper if necessary, then continue cooking for a further 1 to 2 minutes to heat everything through.

Garnish with plenty of chopped parsley and serve with a side salad.

vegetable main courses

Green, red, and golden onions are joined by the sweet white varieties in this choice of vegetable main dishes. Bake onions into pies, force them into ravioli, or chop them into baked potatoes. Onions are essential for flavor-packed vegetable dishes.

cheese and onion *stuffed baked potatoes*

Serves 2

2 large baking potatoes,
   weighing about 8 oz (225 g)
   each
2 red onions, halved
Olive oil
1 cup (250 mL) Cheddar
   cheese, grated
Salt and black pepper
1 Tbsp (15 mL) butter or
   1–2 Tbsp (15–25 mL) milk

Baked potatoes are really special when the centers are scooped out,

mashed, and seasoned – it's worth the extra effort!

Preparation time: 10 minutes Cooking time: 1½ hours

Preheat the oven to 400°F (200°C). Scrub and score the potatoes, then place them in a small roasting pan with the onions. Drizzle the onions with olive oil then bake for 1 hour, or until the potatoes are done.

Slice the potatoes in half and scoop the soft centers out into a food processor. Add the baked onion, most of the cheese, seasonings, and butter or milk and process until smooth in consistency.

Pile the filling back into the potatoes, top with the remaining cheese, and return to the oven for 10 to 15 minutes, or brown lightly under a hot broiler.

baked stuffed *onions*

Serves 4

4 large onions
½ cup (125 mL) bulgur
Salt and black pepper
½ cup (125 mL) boiling
   vegetable broth
1 Tbsp (15 mL) butter

Baked onions make a marvelously comforting food when you are

feeling under the weather. I have kept the filling simple,

so this is an ideal dish for delicate days.

Preparation time: 40 minutes Cooking time: 20 minutes

Preheat the oven to 400°F (200°C). Peel the onions but leave their roots intact. Bring them to a boil in a pot of water and simmer for 15 to 20 minutes, until just tender.

Meanwhile, measure the bulgur into a cup, transfer it to a bowl, and add the same volume of water. Allow to stand until required.

Take the onions out of the pot and run them under cold water until cool enough to handle. Carefully cut around the tops with a very sharp knife, then scoop out the pulp with a teaspoon, leaving a secure shell. The root helps the onions to keep their shape while you are doing this.

Chop the onion pieces. Drain the bulgur, then mix it with the chopped onion and a little seasoning. Pack the mixture back into the onions, and place them in a small, buttered ovenproof pan.

Add the boiling broth, top each onion with a little butter, then bake them in the oven, uncovered, for 15 to 20 minutes until golden brown. Spoon a little of the broth over the onions once or twice during cooking.

cheese and onion stuffed baked potatoes

onion ravioli *with walnut and sorrel sauce*

Serves 2

2 large onions
4 Tbsp (50 mL) olive oil
1 clove garlic, chopped fine
Large pinch ground mace
Salt and black pepper
12 fresh no-cook lasagne
　noodles
1/2 cup (125 mL) chopped
　walnuts
4 oz (125 g) unsalted butter
1–2 Tbsp (15–25 mL) shredded
　sorrel

This is a rich and delicious pasta dish. Serve it as a main course with a simple side salad, or divide into smaller portions and serve as an appetizer.

Preparation time: 30 minutes Cooking time: 10 minutes

Chop one and a half of the onions, then cook them in the olive oil with the garlic and mace until soft and golden brown – about 10 minutes over moderate heat. Add salt and pepper then allow to cool.

Dampen the edges and crosswise along the middle of each sheet of lasagne, one at a time. Place about 1 teaspoon (5 mL) of onions on one end of each noodle, then fold the lasagne over in half and seal the edges to make a ravioli pouch. Leave on a damp dish towel until ready to cook.

Slice the remaining onion and cook it in the pan until golden with any remaining onion filling. Once browned, add the chopped walnuts and the butter. Heat until the butter has melted then keep warm.

Bring a large pan of salted water to a boil. Add the ravioli and cook gently for 3 to 4 minutes, then drain and add to the butter sauce with the shredded sorrel. Season to taste and serve.

onion *moussaka*

Serves 4

2 large onions, chopped
2 Tbsp (25 mL) olive oil
1 lb (500 g) minced tofu or
　other meat substitute
2/3 cup (150 mL) red wine
14 fl oz (398 mL) canned
　chopped tomatoes
2 Tbsp (25 mL) chopped fresh
　oregano
Salt and black pepper
1 Tbsp (15 mL) tomato paste
2 large eggplants, sliced
Olive oil
1 cup (250 mL) ricotta cheese
2/3 cup (150 mL) plain yogurt
1/2 cup (125 g) soft goat cheese
　with garlic and herbs

A vegetarian moussaka which marries the rich flavors of eggplant and onion.

Preparation time: 45 minutes Cooking time: 40 minutes

Cook the onions in the oil in a covered pan until soft, then remove the lid and stir in the minced tofu. Cook quickly for 2 to 3 minutes, then add the wine and cook until it has reduced by half. Add the tomatoes, oregano, seasonings, and tomato paste then simmer gently for 30 to 40 minutes, until rich and thick.

Preheat the oven to 425°F (220°C). Fry the eggplant slices in olive oil, a few at a time, until browned. Drain on paper towels and set aside until required.

Layer the onion sauce and eggplant slices in a buttered, ovenproof pan, finishing with a layer of eggplant. Blend the remaining ingredients together into a sauce, add salt and pepper to taste, and spoon the mixture over the eggplant. Bake in the preheated oven for 25 to 30 minutes, until lightly browned. Serve immediately with a tossed green salad.

onion ravioli with walnut and sorrel sauce

95

cheese and *onion fondue*

Shallots work well in this recipe, providing lots of very good onion flavor without altering the consistency of the fondue much. I purée the shallots, so they blend better into the melted cheese.

Serves 4

2 shallots

2 mild red chiles, seeded

1¼ cups (300 mL) hard cider

Juice of 1 lemon

4 cups (900 mL) Swiss cheese, sliced fine or grated

Salt and black pepper

1 Tbsp (15 mL) cornstarch

2–3 Tbsp (25–45 mL) Calvados, (optional)

French bread and cucumber for dipping

Preparation time: 15 minutes Cooking time: 10 minutes

Roughly chop the shallots and chiles, then blend them to a smooth purée, adding a little of the cider, if necessary.

Bring the cider and lemon juice to a boil, then add the cheese and seasonings. Stir constantly, over low heat, until the cheese melts and starts to bubble.

Blend the cornstarch with the Calvados or a little more cider, then stir it into the fondue. Cook for a further 3 to 4 minutes, until thickened.

Pour the fondue into a warmed dish and set over a table burner to keep warm and melted. Dip chunks of bread and cucumber into the pot to scoop up the cheese.

lentil and *onion lasagne*

Lentils make a satisfying sauce for this vegetarian lasagne. For maximum convenience use lasagne noodles that do not require precooking.

Preparation time: 45 minutes Cooking time: 30-40 minutes

Cook the onions in the oil until softened but not browned, then stir in the zucchini and bell pepper and cook for a further 2 minutes. Add the lentils and tomatoes and stir well. Add the broth and seasonings then bring the sauce to a boil. Simmer for 20 to 25 minutes, until the lentils are soft and the sauce has thickened.

Preheat the oven to 400°F (200°C). Place half the onion and lentil mixture in the bottom of a suitable buttered ovenproof pan and top with half the pasta. Repeat the layers. Mix the ricotta and fromage frais or sour cream together, then season with salt and pepper. Add half the cheese then spread the mixture over the lasagne, topping it with the remaining cheese.

Bake in the preheated oven for 30 to 40 minutes, until the topping is set and lightly browned.

Serves 6

2 large onions, chopped fine
2 Tbsp (25 mL) olive oil
1 zucchini, diced
1 green bell pepper, seeded and diced
³/₄ cup (175 mL) red lentils
14 fl oz (398 mL) canned chopped tomatoes
3 cups (700 mL) vegetable broth
Salt and black pepper
2 Tbsp (25 mL) chopped fresh mixed herbs
8 prepared no-cook lasagne noodles, fresh or dried
1 cup (250 mL) ricotta cheese
1¹/₂ cups (350 mL) fromage frais or sour cream
1 cup (250 mL) grated Cheddar cheese

onion and *bell pepper pizza*

A quick pizza, made with a store-bought pizza base, for days when there is very little time to cook.

Preparation time: 15 minutes Cooking time: 10 minutes

Preheat the oven to 425°F (220°C).

Cook two-thirds of the onions in the oil for 5 minutes over high heat.

Place the pizza base on a baking sheet and top with the cooked onions. Arrange the bell peppers on top then finish with the remaining onion slices. Season well with salt and pepper.

Arrange the mozzarella over the vegetables and top with the olives. Drizzle with a little more olive oil if you wish.

Bake for 10 minutes, until the cheese is just beginning to melt, bubble, and brown. Serve immediately with a green or tomato salad.

Serves 2 to 3

3 large onions, sliced very fine
3 Tbsp (45 mL) olive oil
1 prepared 10-in (25-cm) pizza base
1 red and 1 green bell pepper, seeded and cut into rings
Salt and black pepper
1¹/₂ cups (350 mL) mozzarella cheese, sliced thin
12 black olives

cheese *and onion quiche*

Properly cooked, the much-maligned quiche is delicious. The filling should be just set to wobbly perfection.

Serves 4

6 to 8 scallions, trimmed and chopped fine

1 Tbsp (15 mL) olive oil

½ tsp (2 mL) paprika

1¼ cups (150 mL) sifted all-purpose flour

Salt and black pepper

6 Tbsp (75 mL) butter

1 cup (250 mL) grated Cheddar cheese

3 large eggs, beaten

2 cups (425 mL) milk

Preparation time: 15 minutes Cooking time: 40 minutes

Preheat the oven to 425°F (220°C) and place a baking sheet in the oven to warm.

Cook the white part of the scallions in the oil with the paprika until soft – about 4 minutes over low heat. Allow to cool.

Mix the flour with a pinch of salt then cut into the butter until the mixture resembles fine bread crumbs. Add just enough cold water to make a stiff dough then roll out and use to line a deep 8-inch (20-cm) quiche pan, preferably with a loose base.

Mix the green part of the scallions with the chopped white part and half the grated cheese then scatter over the base of the pastry. Beat the eggs into the milk, season lightly, then pour the mixture over the onions. Scatter with the remaining cheese and sprinkle over a little more paprika.

Place the quiche on the hot baking sheet and cook for 10 minutes, then lower the oven temperature to 375°F (190°C) and cook for a further 25 to 30 minutes, until the filling is just set.

Allow to stand for at least 10 minutes before cutting – quiche should be served either warm or cold.

cheese *and onion turnovers*

Makes 4

1 large potato, weighing about 10 oz (300 g), diced fine

Salt and black pepper

One 13-oz (375-g) package ready-rolled puff pastry

2 medium red onions, diced fine

1½ cups (350 mL) diced Cheddar cheese

2 Tbsp (25 mL) snipped fresh chives

Milk to glaze

Appetizing, quick, and easy – what more could you want from a simple supper dish?

Preparation time: 25 minutes Cooking time: 20 minutes

Preheat the oven to 425°F (220°C). Bring the potato to a boil in a pot of salted water, then simmer for 1 minute. Drain and allow to cool slightly.

Cut out four 6-in (15-cm) circles from the pastry. Mix the potato with the remaining ingredients, then divide the filling among the four pastry circles.

Dampen the edges of the pastry with water, then gather the pastry together over the filling, pressing the edges firmly together to seal. Brush with milk.

Arrange the turnovers on a baking sheet, then bake in the hot oven for 15 to 20 minutes, until the pastry is golden. Serve warm or cold.

cheese and onion quiche

99

cheese, rice, *and onion loaf*

Serves 6

1 cup (225 mL) brown rice

2 large onions, sliced thick

4 Tbsp (50 mL) olive oil

1 red onion

2 zucchini

2 cloves garlic, minced

2 cups (450 mL) whole wheat
 bread crumbs

Salt and black pepper

1 large egg, beaten

1 cup (250 mL) grated Cheddar
 cheese

An excellent vegetarian loaf – a refreshing change from nut loaf or lentil bakes, and delicious served with a spiced fruit chutney.

Preparation time: 45 minutes Cooking time: 45 minutes

Cook the rice in a large pot of water – do not add salt as that will toughen the husk of the rice during cooking – allow about 30 minutes for the rice to cook after it comes to a boil. Drain in a colander, then leave until required.

Preheat the oven to 375°F (190°C). Cook the onion slices in 2 tablespoons (25 mL) olive oil until just softened. Leave until required.

Shred the red onion and zucchini on the coarse grating attachment of a food processor, then cook them in the remaining olive oil until just tender. Turn into a bowl and add the remaining ingredients, mixing thoroughly.

Butter a 2-lb (900-g) loaf pan, about 7 x 3½ x 2½ in (18 x 9 x 7 cm), and line the bottom with baking parchment. Arrange half the onion slices in a layer in the bottom of the pan, then top with half the rice mixture. Make a second layer of onion in the middle of the loaf and top with the remaining rice, packing it down firmly. Cover with a layer of buttered foil.

Bake the loaf in the preheated oven for 40 minutes. Remove the foil and ease the loaf away from the sides of the pan with a thin-bladed knife. Turn the loaf out onto a warmed plate and serve sliced.

french bean *and onion frittata*

Serves 3 to 4

1½ cups (350 mL) fresh or
 frozen French beans

6 to 8 scallions, trimmed and
 sliced

2 Tbsp (25 mL) olive oil

6 large eggs, beaten

2 Tbsp (25 mL) chopped flat
 leaf parsley

Salt and black pepper

½ cup (100 mL) grated
 Parmesan cheese

Similar to a Spanish omelet but lighter as it contains no starchy potato. This is an elegant, summer supper dish.

Preparation time: 10 minutes Cooking time: 20 minutes

Cook the beans in boiling salted water for 4 minutes then drain.

Cook the scallions in the oil in an 8-in (20-cm) nonstick skillet for 2 to 3 minutes, then mix in the beans.

Beat the eggs with the parsley, seasonings, and cheese. Pour the mixture into the skillet, tossing the vegetables carefully to coat them in the eggs.

Cook over very low heat for about 15 minutes, until the eggs are just set. If still runny on top when browned on the base, transfer the skillet to a hot broiler to finish cooking the top. Leave for 2 minutes, then cut into quarters to serve.

blue cheese *and scallion cheesecake*

This is really more of a souffléd quiche, delicious and different.

Serve with lots of green salad.

Preparation time: 30 minutes Cooking time: 40 minutes

Preheat the oven to 400°F (200°C), and place a baking sheet in the oven. Prepare the pastry by mixing the flour and salt in a bowl, and then cutting in the butter until the mixture resembles fine bread crumbs. Mix to a firm dough with cold water, then roll out and line a deep 8-in (20-cm) pan, preferably springform. Chill until required.

Beat the ricotta with the egg yolks and yeast extract, then stir in the chopped scallions, blue cheese, and black pepper. Whisk the egg whites until stiff, then fold them through the mixture. Spoon the filling into the prepared pastry case.

Place the cheesecake in the hot oven and immediately reduce the heat to 375°F (190°C) and bake for 35 to 40 minutes, until the filling is set and golden.

Cool the cheesecake for about 15 minutes then slice and serve warm, with a spoonful of sour cream.

Serves 4 to 6

PASTRY

1¼ cups (300 mL) all-purpose
   flour
Pinch salt
6 Tbsp (75 mL) butter

FILLING

1 cup (250 mL) ricotta cheese
2 large eggs, separated
1 tsp (5 mL) active dry yeast
8 scallions, trimmed and
   chopped fine
1 cup (250 mL) blue cheese,
   crumbled
Black pepper
Sour cream to serve

onion *phyllo pie*

I use a mixture of red and sweet onions to fill this light, summer pie –
just serve with green and tomato salads for great outdoor food.
Do cook this in a tin and not a ceramic pan, or the base will never
begin to crisp. It is very rich, so serve small portions.

Serves 6

4 sweet and 2 red onions,
    sliced
¹/₂ cup (100 mL) peanut oil
1 hot red chile, seeded and
    chopped fine
5 to 6 lime leaves, shredded or
    finely grated rind of 3 limes
1 stalk lemongrass, bruised and
    chopped fine
2 oz (60 g) flaked coconut
Salt
2 Tbsp (25 mL) soy sauce
10 to 14 sheets phyllo pastry,
    depending on size

Preparation time: 40 minutes Cooking time: 40 minutes

Soften the onions in a large skillet in 3 tablespoons of the oil, add the chile, lime leaves, and lemongrass, and cook slowly for 15 to 20 minutes, until the onions are softened. Stir in the coconut, add salt to taste, then allow to cool slightly.

Preheat the oven to 400°F (200°C). Blend the oil and soy sauce together. Arrange most of the phyllo sheets in a buttered, deep 8-in (20-cm) round pan, overlapping the sides of the pan and forming a pastry case at least three layers thick. Brush each sheet with oil and soy sauce to keep them moist.

Press the onion mixture into the lined pan, then cover with two more sheets of phyllo, folded in half. Turn the pastry edges in over the pie, score the top of the pastry with a sharp knife, then brush generously with the remaining oil and soy sauce.

Place the pie on a baking sheet and bake for about 30 minutes, until the pastry is crisp and deep golden brown.

Cool slightly before serving sliced with a stir-fry of mixed vegetables.

onion *and saffron risotto*

The temptation with risotto is to add too many flavoring ingredients.

Resist at all costs! Just the onion and saffron are a perfect combination,

when garnished with the fried garlic.

Preparation time: 10 minutes Cooking time: 30–40 minutes

Serves 4

Set the vegetable broth to a boil, then heat the oil and butter together in a large skillet, add the chopped onions, and cook slowly for 6 to 8 minutes, until softened but not browned. Add the saffron to the boiling broth.

Stir the rice into the skillet and coat it in the onion juices, then add about one-third of the broth. Simmer until absorbed, stirring from time to time, then add half the remaining broth. Continue until all the broth has been absorbed into the risotto, giving a moist, creamy consistency – add a little more broth if necessary.

Meanwhile, heat about 1 in (2.5 cm) of olive oil in a small pan, add the garlic slices and fry until golden brown. Drain on paper towels – keep the olive oil to add to mashed potatoes or to use for frying.

Season the risotto to taste and serve hot, garnished with the fried garlic.

6¼ cups (1.5 L) vegetable broth

2 Tbsp (25 mL) olive oil

1 Tbsp (15 mL) butter

1 large onion and 2 red onions, chopped

Few strands saffron

1½ cups (350 mL) arborio rice

Olive oil to deep-fry

2 large cloves garlic, sliced

Salt and black pepper

onion and *gorgonzola ciabatta pizza*

Serves 2

1 large onion, sliced fine
1 red onion, sliced fine
3 Tbsp (45 mL) olive oil
1 ready-to-bake ciabatta loaf
1 large clove garlic, chopped
  fine
6 to 8 anchovy fillets, chopped
Salt and black pepper
2 to 3 sprigs thyme
1 small red bell pepper, sliced
1 cup (250 mL) Gorgonzola
  cheese, crumbled
Olive oil to drizzle (optional)

The Gorgonzola melts seductively over the onions drawing out the flavors of the

Mediterranean. A crunchy, unusual pizza and a great alternative to tomatoes.

Preparation time: 15 minutes Cooking time: 10 minutes

Preheat the oven to 425°F (220°C). Meanwhile, cook most of the onions in the oil over moderate heat for 10 minutes, stirring occasionally.

Bake the ciabatta for 5 minutes. At the same time, add the garlic, anchovy, seasoning, and thyme to the onions and continue cooking.

Split the baked ciabatta horizontally and spread the onion mixture over the two halves on a baking sheet. Top with the remaining onion and the bell pepper then finish with the cheese. Drizzle with a little olive oil if you wish.

Bake in the hot oven for a further 5 to 8 minutes, until the cheese has melted and is lightly browned, then serve immediately.

vegetable
main courses

spanish *onion omelet*

I first had Spanish omelet when my aunt had a Spanish au pair – we used to

love having Maria look after us and cook for us in the holidays.

Preparation time: 15 minutes Cooking time: 12–15 minutes

Heat the oil in an 8-in (20-cm) preferably nonstick skillet. Add the potato and cook slowly for 4 to 5 minutes, stirring occasionally.

Add the onion and bell pepper and continue cooking for a further 6 to 8 minutes, until all the vegetables are tender. Season well.

Add the eggs and stir them through the vegetables. Cook slowly for about 10 minutes, until the eggs are set. If they are not cooked on top before the bottom is browned finish the omelet off under a hot broiler.

Allow to stand for a minute or two, then serve hot, cut into wedges and garnished with parsley.

Serves 2 to 3

2–3 Tbsp (25–45 mL) olive oil
1 large potato, diced fine
1 large Spanish onion, sliced
   fine
1 green bell pepper, sliced fine
Salt and black pepper
4 large eggs, beaten
flat leaf parsley to garnish

onion *and sweet chestnut casserole*

Serves 4

12 small pickling onions

3 Tbsp (45 mL) olive oil

2 medium leeks, sliced

1 red and 1 yellow bell pepper, sliced

2 cloves garlic, sliced

2 Tbsp (25 mL) whole wheat flour

2½ cups (600 mL) vegetable broth

2 Tbsp (25 mL) light soy sauce

2 to 3 bay leaves

1 lb (500 g) shelled sweet chestnuts

Salt and black pepper

Chestnuts are great cold-weather food and complement both the flavor and texture of onions very well.

Preparation time: 20 minutes Cooking time: 30 minutes

Cook the onions in the oil for about 10 minutes, until soft, sweet, and just starting to brown. Add the leeks, bell peppers, and garlic and cook for a further 2 to 3 minutes.

Scatter the flour over the vegetables and stir well, then gradually add the broth. Bring slowly to a boil, stirring all the time, then add the soy sauce and bay leaves with the sweet chestnuts.

Return to a boil then cover and simmer for 30 minutes. Season to taste, adding more soy sauce if necessary, and serve with mashed potatoes.

sweet onion *and rice bake*

Serves 4

6 Tbsp (85 mL) butter

6 sweet onions, chopped

1 cup (225 mL) quick-cooking long-grain rice

1 cup (250 mL) vegetable broth

1 cup (250 mL) milk

Salt and black pepper

1¼ cups (300 mL) grated Gruyère cheese

In France this is traditionally an accompaniment to plain roast meat, but I think it is a worthy main course in its own right. You need sweet onions for the perfect flavor. If you cut down on the butter, you will need to add extra milk with the rice.

Preparation time: 30 minutes Cooking time: 1 hour

Melt the butter in a large skillet, add the onions, and cook slowly for about 15 minutes, until softened and just lightly golden brown. Meanwhile, preheat the oven to 325°F (170°C).

Stir the rice into the onions, coating it well in all the onion-flavored juices, and cook for 2 to 3 minutes. Add the broth, milk, and seasonings, then bring to a boil and simmer for 5 minutes, to par-cook the rice. The rice should still be quite moist, so add a dash more milk if necessary.

Stir in the cheese, then turn into a buttered ovenproof pan and bake, uncovered, for about an hour, until the top is browned and crisp and the rice is tender. Serve hot.

onion and sweet chestnut casserole

cauliflower *and onion cheese*

Serves 4

1 large cauliflower, cut into
   large florets
1 large onion, cut into
   6 to 8 pieces
Salt
1 cup (250 mL) milk
3 Tbsp (45 mL) butter
3 Tbsp (45 mL) flour
1 tsp (5 mL) Dijon mustard
1½ cups (350 mL) Cheddar
   cheese, grated
Black pepper
2 Tbsp fresh bread crumbs
   (optional)

I made this when my husband had an awful cold.

There's nothing like cauliflower in cheese sauce for comfort food, and onions are said to be an effective cold remedy.

Preparation time: 10 minutes Cooking time: 25 minutes

Place the cauliflower and onion in a saucepan with a pinch of salt and just enough water to cover the vegetables. Bring to a boil, cover, and simmer for 10 minutes.

Scoop the vegetables into an ovenproof serving dish with a slotted spoon, then reserve 1 cup (250 mL) of the cooking water.

Add the milk, butter, and flour to the reserved water in the pan and bring slowly to a boil, stirring all the time. Cook until bubbling and thickened, then add the mustard and half the quantity of cheese. Season the sauce to taste, then pour over the vegetables in the dish.

Mix the remaining cheese with the bread crumbs if using – this gives a crisp topping – then scatter over the dish. Brown under a hot broiler before serving.

festive red onion *spaghetti*

Serves 4

2 red onions, chopped fine
8 to 10 scallions, trimmed and
   sliced on the diagonal
2 Tbsp (25 mL) olive oil
Pinch chili powder
²⁄₃ cup (150 mL) heavy cream
Salt and black pepper
10 oz (300 g) spaghetti, freshly
   cooked
2 tomatoes, seeded and
   chopped
Handful chopped chives

I first served this to vegetarian friends one Christmas - it was a great success.

Add grated Parmesan if you wish, but I don't think it's necessary.

Preparation time: 10 minutes Cooking time: 10 minutes

Cook the red onions and scallions in the oil with the chili powder for 2 to 3 minutes, until just softened. Add the cream, bring to a boil, and simmer for 3 minutes.

Drain the spaghetti, then add it to the onion and cream sauce and mix well. Season to taste.

Stir in the chopped tomatoes and chives just before serving.

onion *and ricotta pastries*

A really quick and easy supper dish that is surprisingly

filling and very comforting!

Preparation time: 10 minutes Cooking time: 25 minutes

Preheat the oven to 425°F (220°C).

Cook the onions in the oil with salt and pepper over medium heat for 10 to 15 minutes, until softened and lightly browned.

Meanwhile, cut the pastry into four rectangles, then make a rim of approximately ¹/₂ in (1 cm) around the edges. Brush the rim carefully with beaten egg or milk, then bake in the hot oven for 10 to 15 minutes, until golden brown.

Beat the yogurt or sour cream into the ricotta with the garlic, Parmesan, and seasoning.

Press the centers of the pastry parcels down with the back of a fork, then divide the cheese mixture among them, spreading it out gently. Top with the onion mixture, then return to the oven for 5 minutes to heat through. Serve immediately.

Serves 4

2 large onions, chopped fine
3 Tbsp (45 mL) olive oil
Salt and black pepper
13-oz (375-g) package ready-rolled puff pastry
Beaten egg or milk to brush
2 Tbsp (25 mL) yogurt or sour cream
1 cup (250 mL) ricotta cheese
1 clove garlic, minced
2 Tbsp (25 mL) freshly grated Parmesan cheese

sweet onion *pie*

Serves 6

3 large sweet onions, such as
  Vidalia, sliced thin
4 Tbsp (50 mL) unsalted butter
¹/₂ tsp (2 mL) grated fresh
  nutmeg
Salt and black pepper
1¹/₄ cups (300 mL) all-purpose
  flour
1 tsp (5 mL) paprika
3 oz (85 g) salted butter
2 eggs, beaten
1 cup (250 mL) milk
²/₃ cup (150 mL) sour cream
¹/₃ cup (80 mL) chopped chives

Sweet onions usually have a white skin and a distinctive, nutty flavor. This pie can be served as either a vegetable main dish or as accompaniment to roast meat, or even fish. The runny filling also makes great gravy! I prefer a top-only crust, but make a double-crust pie if you prefer by doubling the pastry ingredients.

Preparation time: 40 minutes Cooking time: 30 minutes

Cook the sweet onions in the butter with the nutmeg over medium heat for about 15 minutes, until lightly golden. Season well then allow to cool slightly.

Meanwhile, preheat the oven to 400°F (200°C). Mix the flour and paprika in a bowl and cut in the butter until the mixture resembles fine bread crumbs. Add sufficient cold water to mix to a firm pastry dough, then turn out onto a floured surface.

Beat the eggs into the milk, sour cream, and chives, then mix into the onions and turn into a suitable buttered pie dish. Roll out the pastry and use to cover the pie, using any trimmings to make decorative leaves. Make a slit in the pastry lid to allow the steam to escape, then brush with a little milk.

Place the pie dish on a baking sheet – in case of any boil-overs – and bake in the hot oven, immediately lowering the temperature to 375°F (190°C), for 30 minutes, or until the pastry is golden brown. Serve hot.

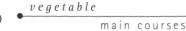

sweet onion pie

sweet onion *and potato tatin*

Serves 4 to 6

3 large sweet onions, such as
   Vidalia, sliced thin
3 Tbsp (45 mL) olive oil
1 small eggplant, sliced
6 to 7 medium potatoes, about
   1¾ lb (800 g), peeled but left
   whole
3 Tbsp (45 mL) butter
1 red chile, chopped fine
Salt, black pepper, and grated
   fresh nutmeg

Based on the classic upside-down apple dessert *tarte tatin*, this is a delicious layered galette of sweet onions, eggplants, and potatoes, spiced with chile and nutmeg.

Preparation time: 40 minutes Cooking time: 40 minutes

Preheat the oven to 400°F (200°C), and place a baking sheet in the oven while it is heating up.

Cook the sliced onions in the oil with the eggplant for about 20 minutes, until all the vegetables are soft and the onions are lightly browned. Cook slowly, over low heat.

Meanwhile, bring the potatoes to a boil in salted water, boil for 5 minutes, then drain and allow to cool slightly. Slice the potatoes thickly.

Melt half the butter in a 9-in (23-cm) deep omelet skillet with an ovenproof handle, remove from the heat, and scatter the chile over the base. Season the onion mixture – adding more salt and nutmeg than pepper, then turn it into the skillet over the chile. Press flat into the skillet.

Arrange the potato slices over the onions, then brush them generously with the remaining butter, melted. Season well.

Bake for 40 minutes, placing the skillet directly onto the hot baking sheet – this will help to caramelize the onions.

Press the potatoes down firmly with a spatula when the tatin comes out of the oven, then loosen around the edges. Invert onto a warmed platter and serve, cut into wedges if possible, although you may resort to spoonfuls, with a salad.

mixed bean *and onion cassoulet*

Serves 6

2 cups (400 g) dried mixed
   beans
1 red, 1 sweet, and 1 large
   cooking onion, sliced thick
3 Tbsp (45 mL) olive oil
Salt and black pepper
4 large sprigs thyme
14 fl oz (398 mL) canned
   chopped tomatoes
About 1½ cups (350 mL)
   vegetable broth
5 cups (1.1 L) fresh bread
   crumbs

This is real winter comfort food – serve it with fresh crusty bread and a green salad.

Preparation time: 1½ hours, plus overnight soaking Cooking time: 1½ hours

Soak the beans in a large bowl of water for 8 hours or overnight. Drain and rinse well in plenty of cold water.

Bring the beans to a boil in a large pot of fresh water, then cover and simmer for 1 hour. Drain and leave until required. Preheat the oven to 325°F (170°C).

Cook the onions quickly in the oil in a flameproof casserole until just soft. Season well, then add the thyme. Pour the tomatoes over the onions, then season them too.

Tip the beans over the tomatoes, pressing them down, then season well. Pour in the broth to come just below the surface of the beans.

Continue heating until the broth just comes to a boil, then cover the casserole and transfer to the oven for 1 hour.

Remove the lid and make a thick layer of bread crumbs over the beans. Raise the oven temperature to 375°F (190°C) and cook for a further 20 to 25 minutes, uncovered, until the bread crumbs are browned.

vegetable side dishes

*Perfect for entertaining or relaxed family suppers, onion side
dishes add zest and color to a meal, as well as introduce
texture and bite. Onion side dishes are usually served hot,
but may accompany hot or cold main dishes.*

roasted endive *with onion*

Serves 4

4 heads Belgian endive
Lemon juice
1 red onion, chopped fine
Salt and black pepper
1–2 Tbsp (15–25 mL) olive oil

I first had endive cooked in this way in Belgium – it has been a favorite vegetable ever since.

Preparation time: 10 minutes Cooking time: 40 minutes

Preheat the oven to 400°F (200°C).

Cut the Belgian endive in half lengthwise and place in a shallow roasting pan. Add a squeeze of lemon juice. Scatter the onion on top, season lightly, and drizzle with the olive oil.

Roast for 30 to 40 minutes, until browned and tender. Serve hot or warm.

singapore-style *onions*

This is a vibrant way to serve onions and a delicately flavored accompaniment to cold chicken or pork.

Preparation time: 15 minutes Cooking time: 30 minutes

Blend all the ingredients for the rempah together in a food processor, adding just enough of the water to make a rough paste.

Fry the shallots in the oil until starting to brown then add the turmeric and cook for a further 1 minute. Stir in the rempah and cook for 2 minutes.

Add the lime leaves or rind and sugar, with most of the remaining water. Bring to a boil then simmer for 10 to 15 minutes, or until the shallots are almost tender.

Blend the coconut milk with the remaining water, add to the pan, and cook for a further 5 minutes. Season with salt and pepper before serving.

Serves 4

REMPAH (CURRY PASTE)

2 to 3 fresh red chiles

1 red onion, chopped

2 cloves garlic, chopped

2 stalks lemongrass, chopped fine

2-in (5-cm) piece ginger root or galangal, peeled and chopped

¼ cup (75 mL) blanched almonds or macadamia nuts

1 cup (250 mL) water

3 cups (500 mL) shallots, peeled and left whole

1 Tbsp (15 mL) peanut oil

1 tsp (2 mL) turmeric

6 lime leaves, shredded or finely grated rind of 3 limes

1 Tbsp (15 mL) raw brown sugar

¼ cup (75 mL) coconut milk or cream

Salt and black pepper to taste

vegetable

glazed *roasted onions*

This is a marvelous onion antipasto, which makes a welcome change from vegetables in oil. The onions may also be served with cold cuts.

Preparation time: 10 minutes Cooking time: 30 minutes

Preheat the oven to 425°F (220°C).

Peel the onions, leaving the root intact, then cut them through in half – the root will hold them together during cooking.

Place the onions, cut side down, in a small ovenproof pan just big enough to take them all. Season lightly, then spoon the remaining ingredients over the onions. Roast in the hot oven for about 25 to 30 minutes, basting occasionally.

Serve the onions warm or cold.

Serves 4

4 sweet white onions, such as
  Vidalia
Salt and black pepper
3 Tbsp (45 mL) orange juice
1 Tbsp (15 mL) balsamic
  vinegar
2 Tbsp (25 mL) olive oil

baked shallots *with garlic bread crumbs*

Serves 4

2 Tbsp (25 mL) olive oil

16 shallots, about 1 lb (500 g)

Salt and black pepper

Pinch ground mace

²/₃ cup (150 mL) vegetable
 broth

4 Tbsp (50 mL) butter

1½ cups (350 mL) fresh white
 bread crumbs

1 clove garlic, minced

Pinch paprika

The subtle flavor of garlic in the bread crumb topping is the ideal

way to finish this simple dish.

Preparation time: 20 minutes Cooking time: 35–40 minutes

Preheat the oven to 375°F (190°C). Heat the oil in a small heatproof casserole, then add the shallots and cook them quickly until browned all over.

 Season the shallots with salt, pepper, and mace, then pour the broth into the pot. Bring to a boil, cover with a lid or foil, and place in the hot oven for 20 minutes, until the shallots are tender.

 Remove the casserole lid and boil away any surplus broth – it should be well reduced to a thickish syrup.

 Melt the butter, add the bread crumbs and garlic and toss them together, adding a little salt, pepper, and paprika for color. Spoon the crumbs over the shallots, then return them to the oven for 10 to 15 minutes, until browned. Serve hot.

champ

A traditional Irish dish which combines potatoes and scallions. I could eat it just as it is, although it is more usual to serve it as an accompaniment.

Preparation time: 10 minutes Cooking time: 25 minutes

Peel the potatoes and cut them into small pieces. Bring to a boil in a pot of salted water, then cover and simmer for 15 to 20 minutes, until tender.

Meanwhile, simmer the scallions gently in the milk for 2 to 3 minutes.

Drain the potatoes, then return them to the pot and place them over low heat for a minute or so, to allow any excess water to evaporate.

Add the milk and onions and pound or beat the potatoes to a soft, fluffy mash. Add plenty of salt and pepper as you go. Mound the champ in a large bowl. Make a little hollow for the butter and allow it to melt into the potatoes before serving.

Serves 4

1³/₄ lb (800 g) potatoes
1 bunch scallions, about 8 to 10, trimmed and sliced fine
²/₃ cup (150 mL) whole milk
Salt and black pepper
8 Tbsp (100 mL) butter

onion, potato, *and bacon rosti*

Serves 4 to 6

6 potatoes, unpeeled, about
  1³/₄ lb (800 g)
6 slices bacon
1 large red onion
Salt, black pepper, and grated
  fresh nutmeg
2 Tbsp (25 mL) butter
2 Tbsp (25 mL) sunflower oil

I have never been successful at rosti – until now! I think chilling the
par-cooked potatoes before grating them has been the answer.

Preparation time: 30 minutes, plus 1-2 hours chilling time Cooking time: 10 minutes

Bring a pan of salted water to a boil, add the potatoes, cover, and boil for 15 minutes.
Drain, then rinse thoroughly under cold water. Chill the potatoes for at least 1 hour in
the fridge – 2 to 3 hours is better.

Chop the bacon finely in the food processor, then fry it until well browned in a
large nonstick skillet.

Meanwhile, chop the onion in the food processor, then fit the coarse grating
attachment. Scrape the skins off the chilled potatoes then grate them into the onion.
Turn into a bowl and mix the crisp bacon into the potatoes and onion with the
seasonings. Shape into 8 flat, round patties.

Heat the butter with the oil in the skillet, then add the rosti mixture. Press down
firmly, then cook over moderately high heat for 3 to 4 minutes on each side. Press the
rosti down firmly again when you turn them. Cook the rostis in 2 batches if necessary,
and serve piping hot.

breads
and bakes

*There are a whole range of breads which can be baked with onions
for extra flavor – chopped fresh vegetables or dried soup mixes will
add an extra taste dimension to your baking, and sliced onions sprinkled
over a loaf make a most attractive garnish.*

pissaladière

Serves 6 to 8

4 cups (400 mL) sliced onions

3 Tbsp (45 mL) olive oil

4 to 5 large sprigs thyme

Salt and black pepper

2 bay leaves

2 cups (450 mL) white bread
flour

½ tsp (2 mL) salt

1 tsp (5 mL) instant dry yeast

2 Tbsp (25 mL) olive oil

2-oz (55-g) can anchovy fillets

8 to 10 black or green olives,
halved

One of my very favorite foods – a pure onion pizza! It's great on its own, but it is also wonderful served in slices with roast beef and vegetables, as an alternative to potatoes. I think it is much better if you stew the onions first to get the juices for making the dough – it takes hours, but it is worth it.

Preparation time: 3½ hours Cooking time: 25–30 minutes

Cook the onions in the oil in a large skillet for 4 to 5 minutes over high heat. Stir in the thyme, plenty of salt and pepper, and the bay leaves, then cover the skillet and allow to stew slowly for up to 2 hours.

Turn the onions into a sieve over a jug and allow all the juices to drain through.

Mix the flour, salt, and yeast together in a bowl, then add the olive oil and the onion juices – you should have about ⅔ cup (150 mL). Mix to a soft, manageable dough then knead thoroughly on a floured surface.

Roll out the dough and press it in a thin layer into the bottom of a pan about 16 x 10 in (40 x 25 cm) – it may not reach quite to the corners, but will spread that way as it rises. Cover with a damp cloth or plastic wrap, and leave in a warm place for about 1 hour, until almost doubled in size.

Preheat the oven to 425°F (220°C). Remove the bay leaves and thyme, then spread the onions over the risen dough. Arrange the anchovy fillets and olives over the onions and drizzle with the oil from the anchovies.

Bake in the preheated oven for 25 to 30 minutes, until the bread base and the onions are browned. Serve warm, cut into fingers.

breads
and bakes

pissaladière

129

ploughman's *bread*

Makes 1 large loaf

2 cups (450 mL) white bread
    flour

2 cups (450 mL) whole wheat
    bread flour

$\frac{1}{2}$ tsp (2 mL) salt

1 tsp (5 mL) instant dry yeast

1-oz (25-g) package dried
    onion soup mix

2 Tbsp (25 mL) olive oil

1 cup (250 mL) grated Cheddar
    cheese

$\frac{2}{3}$ cup (150 mL) beer

About $\frac{2}{3}$ cup (150 mL) warm
    water

1 Tbsp (15 mL) chopped onion
    to garnish

A traditional blend of bread, cheese, onions, and beer – in a loaf! This is almost a meal in itself, but, thickly spread with butter it is delicious with coleslaw and green salad leaves.

Preparation time: 1$\frac{1}{2}$ hours Cooking time: 40 minutes

Mix the flours, salt, and yeast in a large bowl, then stir in the soup mix, the olive oil, and most of the cheese. Make a well in the center and add the beer, then gradually add the water, mixing to a manageable dough.

Turn out onto a floured work surface and knead thoroughly for about 10 minutes, until the dough is smooth and quite elastic. Shape into a loaf and place in a 2-lb (900-g) loaf pan, pressing the dough into the corners of the pan. Cover with a damp cloth or plastic wrap and allow to rise in a warm place for about 1$\frac{1}{4}$ hours, until doubled in size.

Preheat the oven to 425°F (220°C). Mix the remaining cheese with the chopped onion and sprinkle over the loaf. Bake in the hot oven for 35 to 40 minutes. Remove the loaf from the pan. Return the loaf to the oven for 5 minutes, if necessary, to crisp the bottom – it should sound hollow when tapped.

Cool the loaf on a wire rack. Serve sliced, with cheese and salad.

breads
    and bakes

goat cheese *and cinnamon onion rolls*

These rolls, bursting with unusual flavors, are perfect to

serve with soup at a dinner party.

Preparation time: 1³/₄ hours Cooking time: 30 minutes

Cook the onions with the cinnamon in 2 tablespoons (25 mL) of oil in a large skillet for 10 to 15 minutes, until the onions are softened and lightly browned. Season well, then allow to cool.

Mix the flour with the salt and yeast, add the remaining oil, then mix to a soft but manageable dough with the water – adjust the quantity of water as necessary.

Turn the dough onto a lightly floured surface and knead thoroughly for about 10 minutes, until smooth and elastic, then divide into 8 pieces.

Mix the goat cheese with the cooled onions.

Flatten each piece of dough out into a circle and divide the onion and cheese filling among the pieces. Brush the edges of the dough with water, then gather it around the filling. Turn over and roll lightly to a circle about 3 in (7.5 cm) across. Place on oiled baking sheets, cover with damp cloths or plastic wrap and leave in a warm place to rise for about 1¹/₄ hours until roughly doubled in size.

Preheat the oven to 350°F (180°C). Bake the rolls for about 30 minutes until lightly golden. Cool slightly before serving.

Makes 8 large rolls

2 large onions, sliced thin
¹/₂ tsp (2 mL) ground cinnamon
5 Tbsp (65 mL) olive oil
Salt and black pepper
4 cups (900 mL) white bread
  flour
1 tsp (5 mL) salt
2 tsp (10 mL) instant dry yeast
About 1 cup (250 mL) warm
  water
1 cup (250 mL) soft goat
  cheese, crumbled

onion *and pecan bread*

Makes 1 large loaf

2 cups (450 mL) white bread
flour

2 cups (450 mL) whole wheat
bread flour

1 tsp (5 mL) salt

1 tsp (5 mL) instant dry yeast

1 cup (250 mL) pecan pieces,
chopped fine

1 medium onion, grated

1 Tbsp (15 mL) clear honey

2 Tbsp (25 mL) olive oil

1 cup (250 mL) warm milk, or
milk and water mixed

This loaf has a light texture and is allowed to rise twice, even when made

with fast-acting yeast. It is very much a French-style loaf.

Preparation time: about 2 hours Cooking time: 30 minutes

Mix together the flours, salt, and yeast in a large bowl, then stir in the pecans and grated onion.

Beat the honey with the olive oil, then pour it into the flour. Gradually add the milk, mixing to a firm but manageable dough. Turn onto a floured surface and knead thoroughly until smooth – because of the whole wheat flour this dough will not be as elastic as others. Return to the bowl, cover with a damp cloth or plastic wrap, and leave in a warm place for at least 1 hour, until doubled in size.

Punch down the dough and then knead lightly again. Shape into a round loaf and place on an oiled baking sheet. Cover again and leave for 30 minutes.

Preheat the oven to 425°F (220°C). Sprinkle the loaf with a little flour, then bake in the hot oven for about 30 minutes – the base of the loaf will sound hollow when tapped when the loaf is done. Cool on a wire rack before serving.

scottish onion *baps*

These homemade floury milk rolls, called baps in the United Kingdom, are

wonderful, with a soft crust. The perfect roll to hold burgers or salad.

Preparation time: 1¼ hours Cooking time: 15–20 minutes

Mix together the flour, salt, and yeast, then cut in the shortening. Stir in the chopped onions. Mix to a soft, manageable dough with the milk and water, adding a little more warm liquid if necessary.

Turn the dough onto a lightly floured surface and knead thoroughly for about 10 minutes, until smooth and elastic. Divide the dough into 8 and roll out into buns about ½ in (1 cm) thick, placing them onto floured baking sheets.

Cover the baps with damp dish towels or plastic wrap and allow to rise in a warm place for about 1 hour until roughly doubled in size.

Preheat the oven to 400°F (200°C). Dredge the baps with a little extra flour, then bake them in the hot oven for 15 to 20 minutes, until lightly golden. Cool on a wire rack before splitting and serving.

Makes 8

4 cups (900 mL) white bread
  flour
1 tsp (5 mL) salt
1 tsp (5 mL) instant dry yeast
2 Tbsp (25 mL) shortening
1 medium onion, chopped very
  fine
2 scallions, chopped very fine
1 cup (250 mL) warm milk and
  water mixed

onion *seed rolls*

These are great with cheese, cold meat, and pickles. The onion seeds provide

both flavor and a delicious, crunchy texture.

Preparation time: 1 hour 20 minutes Cooking time: 25 minutes

Mix the flour, salt, and yeast together in a bowl, then stir in the soup mix and the onion seeds. Make a well in the center and add the olive oil with enough warm water to mix to a soft but manageable dough.

Turn out onto a floured work surface and knead thoroughly until smooth and elastic – about 10 minutes. Divide into 12, shape into rolls, then place them on floured baking sheets. Cover with damp cloths or plastic wrap and leave to prove in a warm place for about 1 hour, until roughly doubled in size.

Preheat the oven to 425°F (220°C). Dust the rolls lightly with more flour, then bake them in the hot oven for 20 to 25 minutes, until lightly golden. Allow to cool on a wire rack before serving.

Makes 12

4 cups (900 mL) white bread
  flour
1 tsp (5 mL) salt
1 tsp (5 mL) instant dry yeast
1-oz (25-g) package onion
  soup mix
1 Tbsp (15 mL) black onion
  seeds, lightly crushed
3 Tbsp (45 mL) olive oil
1 cup (250 mL) warm water
Flour to dredge

roast red onion and *thyme bread*

Makes 1 large loaf

2 red onions, halved

²/₃ cup (150 mL) extra-virgin
   olive oil

Salt and black pepper

4 cups (900 mL) white bread
   flour

2 tsp (10 mL) instant dry yeast

1 cup (250 mL) warm water

1 Tbsp (15 mL) salt

2 Tbsp (25 mL) fresh thyme
   leaves

Olive oil and coarse sea salt to
   finish

Allowing the yeast mixture to stand for an hour before mixing develops a
slightly sour, authentic Italian bread flavor.

Preparation time: 3 hours Cooking time: 40 minutes

Preheat the oven to 425°F (220°C). Place the onions in a small pan, drizzle with
1 tablespoon (25 mL) olive oil and season well with salt and pepper. Roast in the hot
oven for 45 minutes, allow to cool slightly, and chop fine. Turn the oven off.

Meanwhile, measure 5 tablespoons (65 mL) of flour into a large mixing bowl and
combine it with the yeast and half the warm water – there is no need to mix to a
smooth paste. Cover the bowl with plastic wrap or a damp cloth and leave for 1 hour.

Stir in the oil, salt, and thyme, then add the chopped onion and the remaining
flour. Mix to a soft manageable dough with the remaining water, adding it gradually,
with a little extra if necessary.

Turn the dough onto a lightly floured surface and knead thoroughly for about
10 minutes, until smooth and no longer sticky. Alternatively, knead in a food mixer
fitted with the dough hook.

Shape the dough then press it into an oiled pan about 7 x 11 in (17.5 x 27.5 cm).
Cover as before and leave in a warm place to rise for 1¹/₂ hours, until roughly doubled
in size – this takes longer than usual because of the amount of oil in the dough.

Reheat the oven to 425°F (220°C). Slash the surface of the loaf several times with a
sharp knife, drizzle with extra oil, then sprinkle with coarse salt.

Bake for 35 to 40 minutes until golden. The cooked loaf should leave the pan
easily and be well browned on the base (it's too rich to sound really hollow when
tapped). Cool for at least 10 minutes before eating.

onion and *rosemary focaccia*

This is a classic Italian loaf, made with olive oil and here topped

with sliced onion rings and fresh rosemary.

Preparation time: 1³/₄ hours Cooking time: 30 minutes

Mix the flour, salt, and yeast together in a bowl, make a well in the center, and add the oil and enough water to make a manageable dough.

Turn onto a lightly floured surface and knead the dough thoroughly for about 10 minutes, until smooth and elastic. Roll out the dough then press into an oiled baking pan about 16 x 10 in (40 x 25 cm) – press the dough right up into the corners. Cover with a damp cloth or plastic wrap and leave in a warm place for 1 to 1¹/₂ hours, until well risen and doubled in size.

Meanwhile, soak the onion rings in cold water to soften them.

Preheat the oven to 425°F (220°C). Drain the onion rings and arrange them on the loaf, then sprinkle with the rosemary and salt.

Bake in the preheated oven for 25 to 30 minutes, until the loaf is a pale golden brown and the onions are soft. Allow to cool on a wire rack before eating.

Makes 1 large loaf

4 cups (900 mL) white bread
  flour

1 tsp (5 mL) salt

1 tsp (5 mL) instant dry yeast

¹/₃ cup (80 mL) olive oil

About 1 cup (250 mL) warm
  water

2 large onions, sliced into thin
  rings

1-2 Tbsp (15–25 mL) chopped
  rosemary

Coarse sea salt

spinach and *onion corn bread*

Makes 1 large loaf

1 cup (250 mL) fine yellow
  cornmeal
1¼ cups (300 mL) all-purpose
  flour
2 tsp (10 mL) baking powder
Pinch salt
2 red onions, chopped very fine
1 cup (250 mL) spinach,
  chopped very fine
Black pepper
2 large eggs, separated
⅔ cup (150 mL) milk
⅔ cup (150 mL) heavy cream

An extremely versatile corn bread that is not too sweet.

Quick to mix and bake, this bread may be served hot as an alternative to

potatoes or rice, or cold with cheese or cold meats.

Preparation time: 25 minutes Cooking time: 50 minutes

Preheat the oven to 375°F (190°C), and lightly oil a deep 9-in (22.5-cm) cake pan.

    Mix the cornmeal, flour, baking powder, and salt together, then stir in the onions and chopped spinach with plenty of black pepper.

    Beat the egg yolks with the milk and cream, then pour into the bowl and stir to thoroughly combine. Whisk the egg whites until stiff, then fold them evenly into the onion and spinach mixture.

    Turn the corn bread into the prepared pan and bake in the preheated oven for about 45 minutes, until lightly browned and set.

    Cool the bread in the pan for about 10 minutes before cutting. Serve warm with cheese, or instead of potatoes with a roast.

quick onion and *tomato bread*

Makes 1 loaf

2 cups (450 mL) fine whole
  wheat flour
1 tsp (5 mL) baking powder
½ tsp (2 mL) salt
2 Tbsp (25 mL) chopped parsley
1 red onion, grated
2 tomatoes, skinned, seeded,
  and chopped
2 sun-dried tomatoes, shredded
  fine
2 Tbsp (25 mL) olive oil
1 large egg, beaten
About ½ cup (125 mL) milk

More of a scone loaf than a bread, but an excellent

bake to serve with soup or a winter salad.

Preparation time: 15 minutes Cooking time: 40 minutes

Preheat the oven to 375°F (190°C), and lightly oil a 2-lb (900-g) loaf pan.

    Mix together the dry ingredients with the parsley, then stir in the onion and tomatoes. Add the oil and egg, then enough milk to form a soft dough, but not a wet one.

    Tip the mixture into the prepared pan and press down lightly. Don't bother to smooth the top – it looks better a bit rough! Bake the bread in the preheated oven for about 40 minutes, until golden brown.

    Carefully turn the loaf out of the pan onto a wire rack and cool for at least 10 minutes before cutting.

scallion soda *bread*

This is a marvelous bread to serve with various cheeses at an informal meal.

Makes 1 large loaf

Preparation time: 15 minutes Cooking time: 30 minutes

Preheat the oven to 425°F (220°C) and lightly butter a baking sheet.

Mix the flours in a large bowl with the salt and baking soda, then cut in the butter until the mixture resembles bread crumbs. Stir in the scallions and the buttermilk.

Mix quickly and lightly to a slightly soft but manageable dough – use a spatula and mix with quick strokes. The worst thing you can do to soda bread is overmix it. Add a little extra milk if necessary.

Knead the dough very lightly – just enough to make it into a large round, about 1½ in (4 cm) thick. Place on the baking sheet and mark into 8 sections.

Bake in the hot oven for 30 minutes, until well browned. Allow to cool on a wire rack and serve buttered.

3 cups (700 mL) whole wheat
  flour
1 cup (250 mL) all-purpose
  flour
1 tsp (5 mL) salt
1 tsp (5 mL) baking soda
4 Tbsp (50 mL) butter
6 scallions, trimmed and
  chopped fine
1 cup (250 mL) buttermilk, or
  yogurt and milk mixed

poppy seed and *red onion focaccia*

Makes 1 loaf

4 cups (900 mL) white bread
  flour
1 tsp (5 mL) salt
⅓ cup (75 mL) onion seeds
1 tsp (5 mL) instant dry yeast
2 red onions, grated or chopped
  very fine
3 Tbsp (45 mL) olive oil
1 cup (250 mL) warm water
Olive oil to finish

A seeded, soft bread made with olive oil, with a tang of onion.

Great for lazy Saturday lunches.

Preparation time: 1¾ hours Cooking time: 30–35 minutes

Mix the flour, salt, onion seeds, and yeast in a large bowl, then stir in the onions. Make a well in the center, add the olive oil then add most of the water. Mix to a soft manageable dough, adding more water if necessary.

Turn onto a lightly floured surface, then knead thoroughly until the dough is smooth, elastic, and no longer sticky. Press into a pan about 8 x 12 in (20 x 30 cm), then cover with a damp cloth or plastic wrap and leave in a warm place for 1 to 1½ hours, until well risen and doubled in size.

Preheat the oven to 425°F (220°C). Brush the risen dough with oil, then bake in the hot oven for 30 to 35 minutes, or until the bread is golden and the base sounds hollow when tapped. Cool on a wire rack before cutting into squares to serve.

poppy seed and red onion focaccia

red pesto and *red onion stick*

Makes 1 loaf

1 large red onion, cut into fine rings

2¹/₂ cups (600 mL) white bread flour

¹/₂ tsp (5 mL) salt

1 tsp (5 mL) instant dry yeast

1 Tbsp (15 mL) olive oil

About ³/₄ cup (175 mL) warm water

3 Tbsp (45 mL) red or standard green basil pesto

An unusual bread, great to serve with soup.

The dough is spread with pesto and onions and then rolled so that it

is swirled with color when baked and sliced.

Preparation time: 1¹/₂ hours Cooking time: 30 minutes

Soak the onion rings in cold water until required to soften them.

Mix the flour, salt, and yeast in a bowl, then add the olive oil and enough warm water to make a fairly firm, manageable dough. Turn onto a floured surface and knead thoroughly until smooth and elastic.

Roll and gently pull the dough into a rough oblong shape, approximately 8 x 10 in (20 x 25 cm), then spread it with the pesto sauce.

Drain the onions, shake them dry, then sprinkle them over the pesto. Roll the dough up from one of the long sides, moisten the edge and seal it together firmly. Place the stick on a baking sheet with the seam underneath. Cover with a damp cloth or plastic wrap and leave in a warm place for at least an hour, until doubled in size.

Preheat the oven to 400°F (200°C). Slash the dough diagonally about 6 or 8 times, then bake the stick in the hot oven for 30 minutes, until golden brown. Cool on a wire rack then slice or tear into chunks.

cheese and onion *malted grain rolls*

Makes 12

3 cups (700 mL) malted grain flour

2 cups (450 mL) strong white bread flour

1 tsp (5 mL) salt

2 tsp (10 mL) instant dry yeast

2 red onions, peeled and grated

3 Tbsp (45 mL) olive oil

1 cup (250 mL) warm milk

About ²/₃ cup (150 mL) warm water

1 cup (250 mL) grated Cheddar cheese

Malted grain flour makes a delicious, nut-flavored bread.

I've added some onions and cheese for an extra treat.

Preparation time: 1¹/₂ hours Cooking time: 20-25 minutes

Mix the flours, salt, and yeast together in a large bowl, then mix in the grated onion. Make a well in the center, and add the oil and milk and enough warm water to make a soft but manageable dough.

Turn out onto a lightly floured surface and knead the dough thoroughly until smooth and elastic and no longer sticky.

Divide into 12 and shape into rolls, placing them quite close together on two baking sheets. Cover with damp cloths or plastic wrap and allow to rise in a warm place for about 1 hour, until doubled in size.

Preheat the oven to 425°F (220°C). Sprinkle the rolls with the cheese, then bake in the hot oven for about 20 minutes, until golden and crusty.

Cool on a wire rack.

onion and *buttermilk rye bread*

I first tasted bread similar to this in Poland. It is a dense bread with a deliciously sharp flavor. It contains no white flour, so don't expect it to rise too much.

Makes 2 loaves

4 cups (900 mL) light rye flour, sifted

2 cups (450 mL) whole wheat flour

1 tsp (5 mL) salt

1 tsp (5 mL) nutmeg

7-g sachet instant dry yeast

1 large onion, grated

3 Tbsp (45 mL) olive oil

1¼ cups (300 mL) buttermilk

Milk, rye flour, and onion seeds to decorate

Preparation time: 2 hours Cooking time: 40 minutes

Mix together the flours, salt, nutmeg, and yeast in a large bowl, then stir in the onion. Make a well in the center and add the oil and buttermilk. Mix to a soft but manageable dough, adding a little milk or water if necessary.

Turn onto a lightly floured surface and knead thoroughly for about 10 minutes – the dough will become smooth but not very elastic. Divide into 2 and shape into rounds about 8 in (20 cm) in diameter. Place on oiled baking sheets, then cover with damp dish towels or plastic wrap and allow to rise for about an hour or until roughly doubled in size.

Preheat the oven to 425°F (220°C). Score each loaf into 8 before baking, then brush with milk and sprinkle with flour and onion seeds. Bake in the hot oven for 30 to 35 minutes, until the bases sound hollow when tapped. Cool on a wire rack before cutting and serving in wedges.

onion *pretzels*

Makes 18

1 Tbsp (15 mL) butter

1 cup (250 mL) milk

½ cup (100 mL) water

4 cups (900 mL) white bread
   flour

1 tsp (5 mL) salt

1 tsp (5 mL) instant dry yeast

1 tsp (5 mL) onion seeds

1 egg, beaten

Coarse salt and onion seeds

A really fun bread to make and shape, that children will enjoy helping you make.

Preparation time: 2 hours Cooking time: 20 minutes

Warm the butter in the milk and water until just melted.

Mix the flour, salt, yeast, and onion seeds in a large bowl, then gradually add the liquid, mixing to a slightly sticky dough. Knead thoroughly in the bowl, until the mixture leaves the sides cleanly. Leave the dough in the bowl, cover with a damp cloth or plastic wrap, and leave in a warm place for about an hour, until doubled in size.

Preheat the oven to 475°F (240°C). Knead the dough gently on a lightly floured surface, then divide it into 18 pieces. Roll each one into a thin pencil-shaped log about 12 in (30 cm) long. Lay the roll in front of you in the shape of a horseshoe, then fold the ends up and across, pressing them into the traditional pretzel shape. Arrange on baking sheets and leave for 10 minutes.

Brush the pretzels with egg, then sprinkle with coarse salt and onion seeds. Place in the hot oven, immediately lower the temperature to 400°F (200°C) and bake for 20 minutes, until golden brown.

Cool on a wire rack and serve on their own or with dips.

index

Useful Addresses

W Atlee Burpee Company
300 Park Avenue, Warminster, PA 18974
Toll-Free 1-800-888-1447
Fax Toll-Free 1-800-487-5530
http://www.burpee.com
Walla Walla, Snow Whites and more. Complete on-line catalog.

The Cook's Garden
PO Box 5010
Hodges, SC 29653-5010
Toll-Free 1-800-457-9703
Fax Toll-Free 1-800-457-9705
http://www.cooksgarden.com
Choice selection of onions, sweet and savory, including Giallo di Milano, and the bronzy red Italian Torpedo.

The Gourmet Gardener
8650 College Blvd. Suite 205IN
Overland Park, KS 66210-1806
Tel (913) 345-0490
http://www.gourmetgardener.com
Limited but specialized alliums include Inchelium Red garlic, King Richard and Bleu de Solaise leeks, Red Simiane, Red Beard, and Walla Walla onions, plus the highly demanded French Red shallots.

Ontario Seed Company
PO Box 7 Waterloo
Ontario, Canada N2J 3Z6
Tel (519) 886-0557
Fax (519) 886-0605
Email: seeds@sympatico.ca
One of the largest suppliers of onions to the Canadian market. Most seeds are untreated. No US orders.

Park Seed Co., Inc.
1 Parkton Avenue
Greenwood, SC 29647-0001
Toll-Free 1-800-845-3369
Fax (864) 941-4206
http://www.parkseeds.com
Large seed house offers good selection of onions, including Arkansas, Onion Candy, and Sweet Georgia Brown.

Seeds of Change®
PO Box 15700
Santa Fe, NM 87506
Toll-Free 1-888-762-7333
http://www.seedsofchange.com
Select choice of certified organic, open-pollinated heirloom and traditional varieties. Newburg, Torpedo Red Bottle, Red Wethersfield, Southport, and Valencia onions plus several leeks. Many unusual garlics include Chester Aaron's Certified Organic Rare Planting Garlic used by chefs at famous Chez Panisse restaurant.

Shepherd Garden Seeds
30 Irene Street
Torrington, CT 06790-6658
Tel (860) 482-3638
Fax (860) 482-0532
http://www.shepherdseeds.com
Choice selection includes many onions – Italian Cipollini, White Lisbon Northern Rainbow and Stockton Red – leeks and several varieties of garlic – German Red Rocambole, Gilroy California Late. Garlic chives and French Demi-Long shallots. Free catalog; US only.

Stokes Seeds Limited
39 St. James Street
Box 10 St. Catharines
Ontario Canada L2R 6R6
Tel (905) 688-4300
Fax Toll-Free 1-888-834-3334
http://www.stokeseeds.com
One of Canada's largest seed houses offers almost 40 choices of hybrid white, Spanish and yellow onions, with hybrids suited for particular regions. US and Canada; free catalog.

Terra Time & Tide Seeds
590 East 59th Street
Jacksonville, FL 32208-4824
Tel (904) 764-0376
http://www.seedman.com
Oriental Garlic, Garlic Chives, several bunching varieties (Deep Purple which hold their color) and sweet and savory onions, Redman, Yellow Copra, Pearl Gold Coin, Pearl Jon Purple Skin, Red Burgundy. Argentea leeks and purple-skinned shallots, and seeds for native American varieties: Nodding Onion, Prairie Onion, and Wild Leek. On-line catalog.

The Territorial Seed Company
PO Box 157
Cottage Grove, OR 97424-0061
Tel (541) 942-9547
Toll-Free Fax 1-888-657-3131
http://www.territorial-seed.com
Excellent variety of heirloom and unusual varieties – Egyptian Walking and Catawissa top-setting onions, Pacific Pearl and Long Red Beard scallions, three types of leeks and over 20 garlic, including Korean Red, Purple Italian, and Ukrainian Top Set. On-line catalog.